Out of My Heart And into His

Out of My Heart And into His

Karen Rode

© April 2019, Karen Rode

ISBN: 9781093978605

Printed by Kindle Direct Publishing, an Amazon.com Company

To my husband and children who made my life overflow with blessings

Acknowledgements

I've heard that nobody writes a book alone. After writing this, my first book, I can attest to that. Without the loving input of three people this book would have remained buried in my memory. I shared a snippet of my testimony at a prayer meeting in the home of Dave and Anita Duggan. Anita said, "You need to write your story."

After reading my fledgling first chapters, Coty Sloan phoned me, "You want me to ink this up for ya?" And for the next two years Coty inked up every chapter and every line.

When I had said all I could say, Judith Hensley's expertise in self-publishing brought the manuscript from words on a computer to a book. My heartfelt thanks to you all.

And thanks to my husband and kids for giving me a story to tell.

Disclaimer

To protect their privacy all names have been changed except for members of my family, names of my tour mates on the trips to Ireland and Wales, and Paul Basile, whose wife gave me permission to tell his story.

A Note from the Author

This book is the story of how I sought after God. More definitively, it is the story of how God pursued me, drew me, captured me in the net of His love and changed me into a different person altogether. My story weaves in and out between experiences of body, mind and spirit.

A reader may exclaim as one woman did, "I don't believe it!"

I understand. Sometimes the events of my natural, everyday life contradict the condition of my spiritual life. The only explanation I can give for those discrepancies is that we are complex, triune beings. Sometimes the mind's reasonings and the soul's emotions are not an accurate portrayal of the heart and spirit.

This book chronicles the pilgrimage of my heart and spirit. Like Christian in *Pilgrim's Progress* (a Christian allegory written in 1678 by John Bunyan) I bogged down in sloughs of despond, languished in a prison of despair and fought fierce battles with the giants in my land -- giants of fear, pride, spiritual ambition, and self-hate. My story may challenge credulity at times, but every word is true. I lived it.

Chapter 1 | The Church Basement 13

Chapter 2 | Choosing A Path 18

Chapter 3 | Wars and Rumors of Wars 29

Chapter 4 | Motherhood .36

Chapter 5 | The Redding Years 48

Chapter 6 | The Mission .60

Chapter 7 | Out from The Ashes 72

Chapter 8 | Growing Pains 79

Chapter 9 | A Companion for Control 90

Chapter 10 | Lines Crossed 103

Chapter 11 | Goodbyes .111

Chapter 12 | Love One Another 124

Chapter 13 | Prisoner of War 132

Chapter 14 | The Drifting 141

Chapter 15 | Re-Entry 148

Chapter 16 | Life After Death 156

Chapter 17 | The Wild Atlantic Way 165

Chapter 18 | The Mount 173

Chapter 19 | Molech 180

Chapter 20 | Surprises 188

Chapter 21 | Up from the Wilderness 197

Chapter 22 | This Is What I Know 209

Chapter 23 | Changed .217

The Eleven – Where are they Now? 225

Endnote from the Author 228

References 229

Chapter 1 | **The Church Basement**

I had found what I hoped was a safe hiding place in the basement of my church -- a remote overflow Sunday School room, the one next to the boiler. My back was to the door. I pretended to be busy sorting 3rd grade take-home papers. "Karen," a gentle male voice said. I jumped.

He found me! Unbidden and unrehearsed, one thought rose out of the deepest part of my spirit, *If Joe backs me into a corner, I'll kill him!*

Joseph Williams was an ordinary man, not aggressive, not a threat to anyone. He was a local farmer looking for a wife. I was the right age and a farmer's daughter. Although I had no romantic interest in Joe, I did go out with him a few times out of a sense of Christian duty. His pursuit of me drew him to our small country church and he became a regular attendee. I didn't know if Joe had received Jesus as his Savior. If I rejected his overtures, he might reject church and God and I would be responsible for his eternal damnation in hell. Hence, I felt duty bound to date him.

But there was a problem. I was 23 years old and every date I had ever gone on wrecked me emotionally, no matter who the man or where we went. It always took me days to recover. That Sunday morning, I didn't have days. I had hours because I had gone to a movie with Joe the night before. Twelve hours was not enough time to gather my roiling feelings and stuff them back into a hollow in my being. That's why I was hiding, hoping against hope Joe wouldn't seek me out.

If he backs me into a corner, I'll kill him.

I was horrified. Kill him? Why would I think that? Nothing had happened on that date or any other date to produce such inner terror. No man had ever threatened me, much less harmed me. On the contrary, growing up on a farm in eastern Washington I had enjoyed an idyllic and safe childhood. I was blessed with a loving family - a dad, a mom, two brothers and a sister. Best of all, my grandparents lived a quarter mile up the road.

My grandfather bought horses for us - such a gift for horse-loving me. He won the Greatest Grandpa ever award when he took my brother and me on an overnight camping trip by horseback to nearby Kamiak Butte.

Grandad drove his camper to wilderness areas in search of good fishing. And the fish laughed at his efforts. He probably never caught more than a dozen or so fish on each trip, but he kept trying.

Grandad told corny jokes and laughed heartily at his own pranks. I found out how accurate his aim was with a cow's teat when I peeked through a knothole watching him milk and a stream of the white, warm liquid hit my eye.

When asked what he was doing as he sat by the farm elevator waiting for the harvest trucks to pull in Grandad replied, "Oh, I'm just sittin' here rearranging my prejudices."

My grandmother baked. Her specialties were homemade bread, cracked wheat rolls and gooey cinnamon buns. Soft molasses cookies are an art form and Mama King had perfected it. Friends and family relied on her comfort food to make every gathering special and she never disappointed.

To top it off, when I was a little girl Mama King read to me by the hour -- Grimm's fairy tales, adventure stories, and every story in the Childcraft set of books she owned.

My mom was a typical farm wife, filling her pantry and freezer with produce from her garden and berry patch. She made cottage cheese and ice cream and taught me to bake bread and dress chickens. She supervised my piano practice and supported my school activities. As I grew more proficient on the piano, we played duets in church, Mom on the organ and me on the piano. We laughed much as we played music together, picked berries, canned peaches, cut corn off the cob for freezing and fried fresh killed that morning chicken to take to hungry men in the harvest field.

I adored my father and poured out my affection in hugs and kisses. One wintry evening when I was six-years-old Dad carried me to the car so I wouldn't get my patent leather shoes wet in the snow.

I remember thinking, *I hope I never get too old for my Daddy to carry me.* My safe place was in the arms of my daddy. But life moves on and I did get too old for my Dad to carry me.

It was then that my terror of men began to surface. Like every teenage girl I dreamed of dating and boyfriends, but my excitement and anticipation on the few dates I had in high school and college could not cover my fear. My panic manifested in uncontrollable physiological reactions. On every date I held my body rigid to keep from trembling while rivulets of perspiration ran down my arms. When my muscles could no longer hold steady in that contracted state, I shuddered involuntarily. One boy quipped to my brother after a date with him that I sat in the crack between the passenger door and the seat, as far away from him as possible.

What is wrong with me? Why am I so afraid? Why am I such a mess?

I could not unravel the mystery of my own soul. That Sunday morning with Joe elevated my problem to a crisis status. Something had to be done.

How does one account for such a mystery? From time to time there are behaviors or talents or passions in an individual's life that defy logic. A look at generational influences offers one explanation of these enigmas. We often observe musical talent, artistic gifting or business acumen passed down in a family, or sometimes skip a generation. Contrarily, alcoholism, broken homes or criminal behavior may infect a family generationally like a disease embedded in the DNA.[1]

I can't say with certainty what happened in my generational line to trigger my terror of men, but two possibilities come to mind. In my twenties I had a vision in which I was standing in front of my mother's grave knowing men had killed her. I felt the grief and anguish of that loss as though it were true, even though my mother was actually alive and well. A few months later I read a magazine article detailing how a Mafia man tortured his wife as punishment for committing adultery. She died days later.

Both my vision, and this article lodged in my mind.

Traumatic events such as these occurring in my generational line and passed down to me could explain my fear of men. Regardless of its origin the phobia was there, and I would have to deal with it.

When I stood in the corner of that church basement, gripped with a terror so overwhelming I was prepared to commit murder, I didn't know that my life would be marked by the relentless pursuit of a loving God. All I knew was that my soul was wounded, and I needed help. I needed help beyond quick fix personality techniques. I needed real, radical, lasting, transformative change. I needed change that would reconstruct the spiritual DNA of my heart and spirit. In a word, I needed God.

Chapter 2 | **Choosing A Path**

From my earliest memory I hungered after God. Raised in a Christian home, I was baptized when I was eight years old and attended Sunday school and church every week. At age sixteen I had a bona fide born-again experience at a Baptist youth retreat. My hunger for God continued to increase and two years later I received the baptism of the Holy Spirit.

In 1971, friends invited me to deliverance meetings being held in Spokane, Washington by Pastor Ben Stockman. Ben traveled the country from his base in Fresno, California teaching and ministering freedom from fear, sorrow, anger, lust, doubt, "death powers" as he called them.

I experienced my own release from fear and anger in Pastor Ben's meetings and continued pursuing inner freedom with occasional phone counseling sessions. In one session I shared with Pastor Ben my plan for holiness. My ambition, I declared, was to be a genderless ethereal being floating around blessing people, much like an angel in disguise. Reading the Apostle Paul's writings in 1st Corinthians 7 about the benefits of a single life gave me the idea that celibacy devoted to God scored higher on the scale of holiness than married life.

This viewpoint aligned itself perfectly with my growing passion for God and my ever-growing distrust of men. I wanted to go to heaven, and everyone knows heaven is for the pure. A single life of sexual abstinence would earn a shining badge of purity for me and assure my entrance through the pearly gates. Even though I had been taught rightly that salvation is not earned by good works but paid for and given freely through the death of Jesus Christ, now I had a back-up plan. A single life, especially one devoted to overseas mission work, guaranteed accolades here on earth and a red-carpet entrance into heaven.

I graduated from Whitworth College with a bachelor's degree in secondary education, trained to teach at the junior high and high school level. It was unfathomable to me that anyone could pursue a career in elementary education. My younger brother and sister are eleven and twelve years younger than me and I functioned as chief babysitter and fun maker for them. But by the time I reached college I viewed young children as creatures from outer space. How could one even communicate with such mysterious, unformed intellects, much less teach them anything?

These vacuum areas in my spirit with regards to men and children began to be uncovered in high school and college. This rejection of a large segment of the human race makes no sense unless viewed in the context of unknown generational influences passed down to me. I couldn't imagine teaching any grade lower than seventh grade and fully intended to earn a master's degree immediately after graduation so I could teach at the college level. Counsel from a professor stopped me. He advised me to wait a few years and acquire experience in the classroom first so I would have a better idea what direction to take for further studies.

    I believe this was divine intervention. If I had gained a master's and doctor's degree, I could easily have become so embedded, even petrified, in the mindset of education that I would not have heard God's call to a different life.

    Having received the highest recommendations given to a student teacher I confidently pursued my goal of holiness through full-time Christian service by applying to a mission board to teach English in a foreign country. I was rejected. The denomination's mission board did not embrace my charismatic experience and felt I was not a good fit for their program. My pursuit of holy singleness may have suffered a slight setback, a detour of sorts, but I continued my quest. In the meantime, I accepted a job teaching 8th grade English and history in the Spokane Valley school district.

    Sex was a large factor fueling my search for holiness. I observed the devastation and pain people, even little children, suffer due to the corruption of sexual function. I concluded that God was wrong to create an ability with so much potential for evil. Obviously, God hadn't thought this thing through very well. I felt He should admit His mistake, apologize to mankind and fix it. I couldn't wait around for God. I needed an immediate remedy. I would be a spiritual *it*, floating around blessing people. All I needed, I told Pastor Ben during a counseling session, was to be delivered from those pesky woman feelings — the ones that made me desire a man and marriage.

To my surprise Pastor Ben did not applaud my lofty ambition. Instead, he thundered, "God didn't make any *its*. He made you a woman and you will only be fulfilled as a woman."

Sarah, Rachel and Hannah, Pastor Ben continued, are held in high regard in scripture because they desired children. God answered their longings and their requests. They bore Isaac, Joseph and Samuel, each of whom God used mightily. The Bible honors these women as examples of faith and holiness to be emulated.

Pastor Ben proceeded, "For every function of man God created there are three options: misuse, disuse and right use."

The world's misuse of sexual function so appalled me I intended to employ disuse. It was possible, Pastor Ben assured me, to experience sexuality as God intended — pure, healthy and wholesome. Further, he explained God's first commandments to man were to be fruitful and have dominion. Nowhere in scripture have those commandments been altered or rescinded. They are primal, foundational, part of the fabric of creation, and express what God views as important.

These ideas challenged me. I wrestled all night in prayer. Could I, from my heart, embrace God's priorities? In answer to my question about sex God brought to my mind Peter's vision of unclean animals and made it personal, "Call not unclean anything I have cleansed" (Acts 10:15). God created sexual function and I disobey His command to label it "unclean."

In the early morning hours, I handed over my ethereal *it* fixation, praying, "Not my will, but Yours be done." That decision opened the door to full-time Christian service beyond anything I could have imagined.

Shortly after the Joe incident Pastor Ben invited me to move to Fresno, California and join the office staff of his ministry and I accepted. During a phone call a few days before I left for California he ventured, "There's a man who comes to the Saturday night prayer meetings I think you should meet. His name is Howard. He's been preparing himself for a wife and you've been preparing yourself for a husband. You've made a decision to embrace and walk in God's original purpose for man and woman. God may intend to join you two in marriage."

I did not feel pressured by Ben's suggestion, rather, I felt forearmed. However, making a commitment to God as I did that night on the floor of my bedroom was one thing, but facing a working out of that decision was quite another and the facing was immediate.

On my arrival in Fresno on a Sunday afternoon, I got out of my car at the ministry headquarters. Standing on the sidewalk, as I was getting my bearings on these new surroundings a man strode around the side of the ministry's office and headed straight for me.

Feet, do not move!

Only with concentrated effort, mentally nailing my feet to the sidewalk, could I keep from shuffling backwards. If tall, dark and handsome describes the perfect man, this guy was perfect. I took in his friendly grin, near black hair and trim physique.

"Hi, I'm Howard."

My eyes approved, but no amount of window dressing could cover the fact that Howard was a man. The scene with Joe was still fresh in my mind. I didn't know how to function in God's world of men and women.

Mercifully, Howard shortly left for his home in Lodi and I drove to the ministry staff house located a mile from the office. I was grateful Howard lived two hours away. It meant a reprieve until Saturday night's prayer meeting.

A few days later I attended a gospel concert at a local church. In my small country church, I played piano, arranged music and sang in a ladies' trio. I longed to be part of a gospel singing group and travel around the country performing in churches.

Halfway through the concert the leader of the group announced, "We're looking for a singer and piano player to replace my wife who is eight and a half months pregnant."

My heart pounded. My mind raced. *Is this a chance to fulfill my musical dream? I could travel with a Gospel group and escape a frightening relationship with a man, all with one decision.*

As I frantically pondered this possibility God answered my question with a vision. A gossamer curtain scrolled down between me and the singers on the stage. It was if a screen hung in front of my eyes on which God played a movie. Being a visual person, visions speak powerfully to me and I believe that is why the Lord often uses them to direct my path. On the right side of this gossamer curtain was a desert scene. Dry, barren, nothingness. On the left side Howard stood in a lush, tropical garden, his eyes pleading, "Come and help me."

My heart broke. I had vowed before God to embrace His priorities of fruitfulness and responsibility. A clear-cut choice was laid before me. Barrenness, choosing my own path or fruitfulness, choosing God's path. Would I do it? Would I choose the fruitful path even though it meant laying down a cherished dream and facing an uncertain future? I was afraid but my devotion to God's will and the cry of this man's heart compelled me to respond, "I will."

In the weeks that followed, thoughts of Howard filled my mind. We had exchanged the briefest of "hellos" and I saw him at group prayer meetings.

I complained to God, "You're asking me to buy a 'pig in a poke.' I don't know this man."

God replied, "It wouldn't matter how well you knew Howard — you wouldn't know his heart. I know his heart and I'm telling you Howard is My choice for you."

Then it happened. The thing that I greatly feared came upon me (Job 3:25). After a Saturday night prayer meeting Howard asked me out to dinner the next day, April 23, 1972.

I had to say, "Yes," even while fear throttled my heart and mind. The next afternoon I dressed for the date and shared my distress with the ladies at the staff house. They prayed with me as I covered my face with my hands.

One of the women gently removed my hands. "You don't have to wear a mask anymore," she said.

I don't have to cover my brokenness and attempt normalcy? To even consider the possibility brought a tiny measure of calm to the hurricane of emotions within.

Howard took me to Pardini's restaurant and suggested we both order his favorite meal — prime rib. I had never eaten prime rib. It was melt-in-your-mouth delicious and halfway through dinner Howard commented, "This is kind of a birthday celebration."

"Yes, it is," I replied. *How does he know my birthday?*

Howard continued, "My birthday is tomorrow, April 24th."

"Mine is on the 25th!"

It was pretty funny, especially later when Howard shared with me his wish list for a wife which he had compiled a few years prior. Topping the list of eight or ten specifications was "a woman fourteen years younger than me." When Howard wrote his list, he felt the Holy Spirit endorsed his peculiar request. He wanted to marry a younger woman with whom he could have children. Howard was thirty-eight years old on that first date, and I was twenty-four — fourteen years and one day younger.

I don't recall all the items on Howard's list, but I was a match for most of them. Howard desired a wife of German heritage. Both his parents emigrated to the United States from the Ukraine as part of a large German influx when they were very young. I'm not purebred like Howard, but there is German blood in my lineage. Howard played tuba, so he thought it would be nice if his wife played piano.

I played piano, check. Singer, check. Cooking abilities, check.

Howard's testimony was that he fell in love with me at first sight. The fact that I came "fully loaded" with nearly all the attributes he wished for in a wife confirmed me to him.

Pastor Ben joked, "When Karen showed up Howard bought the goods before the store was even open."

I, however, had a closet full of fleeces ready to be laid out. One came at a prayer meeting. Growing up, Howard suffered from fear and insecurity. During his teenage years he looked to his dad, a successful businessman and property owner, to teach him how to be a man. In Howard's eyes his dad was everything he was not, and Howard believed he needed his dad to confirm and establish his fledgling manhood. It was not to be. Dad Rode died in an automobile crash when Howard was 17 years old.

It was a terrible blow and Howard had never given himself full license to grieve. That night in the prayer meeting God opened Howard's hidden reservoir of unshed tears and he lay on the floor weeping. My heart broke for him. I wanted to help. Pastor Ben observed my outreach to

Howard that night and remarked later that he knew then I had joined myself to Howard.

Pastor Ben was convinced, Howard was convinced, but I required more. God instructed me to read all four Gospel accounts of the crucifixion of Jesus. By the time I reached, "When Jesus had received the sour wine, He said, 'It is finished' and He bowed His head and gave up His Spirit" (John 19:30 AMP). I was reeling inside. No flimsy, flim-flam, ambivalent commitment to God and His will, would do--His will that included Howard. This was an all-or-nothing proposition.

God, if I choose this path, it will cost me everything.
"When has it ever cost any less?" He replied.

I recalled the words of pastor and theologian, Dietrich Bonhoeffer, "When God calls a man, He bids him, 'Come and die.'"

Marriage is a come and die moment for everyone. Entering that covenantal relationship requires that two uniquely fashioned individuals give up certain rights and privileges of the independent life. They choose to live life together as one believing that what they can create in their union is greater than what they would achieve in singleness. I knew that this call from God to marry Howard, or any man, meant that I would need to die to self in a measure I had not experienced previously.

One final fleece would be laid out. I flew to Wheaton, Illinois to attend a writer's conference. The keynote speaker at the closing banquet was a single woman, a company vice-president. She spoke of her many opportunities and successes in sharing her faith with fellow travelers and business professionals as she traversed the globe. Her testimony made her life sound so valuable, so important, so evangelistic, so exciting. It was the kind of life I had desired for a long time.

As this woman spoke the Holy Spirit showed me her inner life and spirit. I saw a dry twig. The image was a sharp contrast to the outward success she was describing, but I believed God was showing me that things on the outside are not always as they seem when it comes to matters of the heart. As in the vision at the church, God juxtaposed barrenness and fruitfulness. Perhaps for that woman her lifestyle was indeed fruitful, but if I tried to emulate her, it would be a dry twig.

I imagined myself capable of being a charismatic, unmarried college professor inspiring, and wowing students with my sharp wit and intellect. I could attempt to bring that imagined life to pass. But if my desire was for inner fruitfulness the path for me was marriage and children.

My closet full of fleeces was now empty, my heart persuaded. I couldn't wait to fly home and into Howard's arms. Passion for the will of God overrode my fear and I wanted to put as much distance between myself and a barren lifestyle as quickly as possible. So, I followed the Biblical example of Ruth and proposed to my future husband upon my return.

"Howard, let's get married," I gushed.

And so, we did. On July 16, 1972, four months after we met, Pastor Ben performed our marriage ceremony on a hilltop in Lewiston, CA with a few friends present. We honeymooned at a relative's cabin in Lake Tahoe and settled into Howard's small house in Lodi, California.

"No man having put his hand to the plough, and looking back, is fit for the kingdom of God" (Lk. 9:62 KJV). Though I was convinced marriage to Howard was God's will, still I looked back wondering if I had chosen something less than total commitment to Christ. In my mind lingered the thought that a single life of sacrificing on the foreign mission field rated higher on the scale of a sold-out disciple of Jesus than marriage and family living comfortably in the United States.

The Lord severed that last thread of doubt that bound me to the past when Howard and I attended a missionary convention held in his home church in Lodi.

The guest missionary shared, "My mother wanted to be a missionary and was disappointed that it did not work out for her. But she raised four sons. Three of us are missionaries and my brother is a pastor. Her longing to serve God was multiplied in her children."

Chapter 3 | **Wars and Rumors of Wars**

Marriage often uncovers secret doors and passageways, areas hidden until exposed by the pressures of a joined life. I, and those who knew me, thought of me as an emotionally stable person not easily angered. I thought of myself as being incapable of full on 'see red' rage. That was before I married Howard. I not only found myself quite capable of anger, but with fear adding oxygen to the flame, I would come to discover what it felt like to be engulfed in fury.

Sometimes fear manifests itself in self-defense and anger. Fear torments (1 John 4:18). In order to assuage the torment of fear, the soul overlays the anxiety with anger. This gives the suffering person a sense power and control over the circumstances that are producing the terror. In the early days of our marriage, this was how I coped.

Shortly after Howard and I were married, God revealed to me in a vision the intensity of fear and anger residing in my soul. In this vision I was dressed in gleaming armor like Joan of Arc and I sat astride a horse on top of a mountain. Jesus sat astride a white horse beside me. In the valley below stood all the men in the world.

I turned to Jesus and in all sincerity offered, "You want me to go down there and wipe them all out for You, Lord?"

I assumed Jesus had as much trouble with men as I did and would be glad of my offer to rid the world of this problem of males. I felt strong and confident, fully capable of accomplishing the task single-handedly. Jesus didn't answer me.

As startling as this vision was, I knew it was true. Since being married I had been having nightmares: men were after me to kill me. Projecting my heart thoughts onto men my subconscious mind concluded if I wanted to kill men, then they, in turn, wanted to kill me. Embracing the axiom that the best defense is a good offense the law of self-preservation within me believed my response to men was kill or be killed.

One nightmare was particularly frightening. I was running through dark fields to escape from a man who was chasing me. Racing to a cluster of old sheds, I hid under a wooden platform. Just like Joe, my pursuer searched until he found me. He reached for me.

I awoke, frozen with fear, afraid to move, even breathe. Howard lay beside me in the bed. I wanted to reach out and touch him, but I was too paralyzed to move. Howard stirred and rolled over. His arm came around me pulling me into an embrace. With one somnolent action, I was rescued from that cold, night terror into the warm and safe fortress of his arms. Love drove out fear. My nightmares ceased. I never had another one.

Despite some victories, I was consistently

confronting storms in my spiritual life and culture shock in my natural one. Separated from my family and my past, I had barely begun on this new path when I became pregnant with our first child. Howard was elated. He trumpeted, "His name is Samuel," even though he did not know if the baby was a boy or girl.

Since fruitfulness was my chosen priority, I was not surprised that I conceived with child within weeks of our marriage. Though I was interested in the physical change pregnancy was making in my body, I did not have an emotional connection with this baby as Howard did. At the time I did not think that unusual. I was juggling my emotions and perceptions, trying to adapt to the many changes in my life. God would soon reveal the cold vacuum in my heart regarding motherhood.

As we navigated married life, Howard and I agreed on major issues like religion, frugality, and what to eat. We both came from middle class backgrounds. What was there to fight about? Money, for one.

Howard gave me grocery money with the injunction, "Make it go as far as you can."

Every week I bought a whole chicken, roasted it, served two or three meals from it, then boiled the bones and made soup. There's nothing wrong with extracting every gram of nutrition from a chicken. The problem lay with my fear. Fear prevented me from asking Howard for more food money. I generated anxiety over grocery shopping and meal preparation.

Furthermore, Howard talked incessantly about money and his perceived lack of it. My dad and mom had never discussed money in front of me and never expressed worry over money. The only time I knew we were tightening our belts is the year my mom meticulously recorded every expenditure. Howard's incessant monologues about money stirred up more fear in me.

"Any job worth doing is worth doing well."

Howard was a poster child for that proverb. He brought a perfectionist's zeal to every task. Perfection was not my goal in the ordinary chores of life. My goal was FUN! Life is composed of many boring and mundane duties. My remedy was B.Y.O.F. — bring your own fun. I learned that lesson from my Mom. We had laughed our way through picking berries, canning peaches, cooking meals, making root beer and cleaning the house. We didn't worry about perfection because a job well done with joy was an accomplishment to be proud of.

Howard couldn't have disagreed more. Frivolity distracted him. He needed space and quiet to concentrate and he believed no one could do superior work without following his protocol. Everything was to be done soberly with forethought, accuracy and precision.

"Do you hang the toilet paper so that it comes off the top of the roll or the bottom?" Howard innocently asked me.

Who cares? I thought.

"It doesn't matter. Top or bottom. Whichever way it lands."

Incomprehensible to Howard. He informed me that we would standardize and always hang the toilet paper, so it came off the top of the roll. Such a minuscule detail, yet it portended constraints that I found limiting and confining.

One evening I finished washing the dishes and draped the dishcloth over the sink to dry. I was relaxing in the living room when Howard insisted I return to the kitchen. He demonstrated how much more water he could wring out of the dishcloth by folding it precisely in fourths and twisting vigorously. My sloppiness, he contended, would result in a smelly dishcloth.

I knew how to cook, bake bread, dress chickens, make root beer, plant a garden, can and freeze fruits and vegetables. Many of my clothes I made myself using challenging designer patterns. I sewed the slacks and shirt Howard wore for our outdoor wedding as well as my country-style wedding dress. Correspondence writing courses had given me the skills to write two articles that were published in national magazines. Everyone who knew me thought my resume long and impressive. But under the exacting eye of Howard's perfectionism, my self-confidence began to erode.

When I introduced Howard to my church friends one lady embarrassed me by accosting Howard with, "I hope you're good enough for Karen."

I was proud of my husband's answer, "We're both trying to be good enough for Jesus."

Howard was glad to have me, but in his view, I was not a finished product. Rather, I was prime raw material that his expertise could shape into what he unconsciously desired — a duplicate of himself in everything natural. Howard's talent in organizing and upgrading his physical environment justified, in his mind, his propensity to control everything and everyone. The world would be a logical and efficient place if everyone conformed to Howard's way of doing everything. Maddeningly, to some degree, he was correct. The dishcloth experiment was proof enough of the efficacy of Howard's well thought out, reasoned ways in all things practical.

We were only a few weeks into our marriage and in household details Howard didn't seem to think I did anything right. I couldn't even hang shirts on a clothesline correctly. My mother taught me how to hang shirts and every woman I knew agreed with her method. You hang shirts from the hem, so the clothespin does not crinkle the top of the shirt.

Howard cared not a whit for what any woman thought. He reasoned you hang shirts from the collar. The moisture from the collar and yoke drain to the single fabric of the shirt and it dries faster. After all, the objective is to dry the shirt. Howard's position on this, as in so many things, was unyielding. This shirt debacle was the straw that broke the back of my resolve to be a submissive wife.

I had never met anyone like Howard. My free spirit felt squelched, unappreciated. I fought back, trying to regain the image of my exalted self. But I was stunned and numbed, shut out and shut down by Howard's dominant personality. The very small, molehill details of living together became mountains for Howard to establish his absolute rule. War was brewing.

My fear was gearing up to battle against Howard's control — a head on collision between the irresistible force (me) and the immovable object (Howard). The coalition of my fear and pride made assault after assault on Howard's tower of perfectionism and control. It was impenetrable. We were at a stalemate. But I was no longer looking for stalemate. I had become vindictive. I wanted checkmate.

How can I level this tower? How can I regain control? How can I really hurt Howard? My fury was fertile ground for a horrendous thought. *The way to really hurt him is to abort his child.*

In my mind this new life was "Howard's child," not "ours." I was eight weeks along in my pregnancy and I had no natural, maternal feelings for the baby growing inside me.

Having an abortion was out of the question, but if my mental aggression towards Howard somehow triggered a miscarriage, who could fault me? It happened all the time, right? It would deal Howard a crippling blow from which he would not recover. It would bring him, if not under me, at least on equal footing in our battles for supremacy.

In the prayer room of our church God wiped my chessboard clean from that conflict between Howard and I. Pastor Ben walked in as I was alone and seeking God. He began to sing in the Spirit. It was a lullaby in an unknown language. Another vision. It was as if I sat in a movie theater beside the Holy Spirit. The lights dimmed and the screen filled with the opening scene — a panorama view set in the old West of the United States. The landscape was quite level and barren with only a smattering of greenery here and there. The camera zoomed in to a small sod house surrounded by dust, the effects of drought.

A scraggly tree stood on the knoll a short distance from the house and a woman sat in a rocking chair under the tree. She wore a threadbare house dress and had a baby in her arms. She rocked and crooned contentedly to the babe swaddled in a tattered blanket. The sun was setting, and the woman was waiting for her husband to ride over the hill, coming home for dinner.

In contrast to the obvious physical poverty, to me the scene portrayed richness. It was rich in peace, joy, love, and especially, contentment. I wanted to be in that scene. I wanted to be that woman filled with such peace and contentment, such joy in being a wife and mother that she thought there was no better place on earth than sitting under that scraggly tree, rocking her baby waiting for her husband to come home to eat dinner together in a one room sod house.

Chapter 4 | **Motherhood**
"The Lord is my Shepherd. I shall not fail."

The prospect of parenthood united Howard and me. Nevertheless, rocky roads lay ahead. God gave me Psalm 23 as His rock to stand on, especially the first verse, "The Lord is my Shepherd; I shall not want" (Ps. 23:1). *Want* can also be translated *lessen, fail, lack.* The Lord promised I would not fail.

I was proud of the accomplished person I perceived myself to be before marriage to Howard. The cure for pride is humility.

James exhorts, "Humble yourselves before the Lord, and He will lift you up" (James 4:10 New International Version). God knew I was unable to humble myself, so He enacted Daniel 4:37 (NIV). "Those that walk in pride he is able to humble," and He used Howard to do it.

Living with Howard I felt devalued, stripped of who I was as a single woman. When Howard and I married I had $1,800 in my bank account. The funds were enough to pay off Howard's recently purchased car, saving us from future interest charges. He asked to use my earnings for that purpose. I'm a practical person and believe in saving money so I said, "Yes," not realizing until later that my inner self would perceive that as another loss. That money represented "me," my labor, my life force, and, in a flash, it was gone.

In addition, the activities and accomplishments that made me feel important in the past seemingly held no significance in this new life. I wanted to soar in the heavenlies with grand thoughts and important ideas. Howard wanted me to join him in perfecting the minutiae of our natural habitat.

A few months before Samuel's birth we moved to Fresno, California and Howard started a handyman business. As a teenager he learned how to fix almost everything working on his dad's rental properties. Howard was extremely gifted in all things mechanical. He had an uncanny ability to pinpoint the problem in an appliance, plumbing leak or electrical circuit. He performed light carpentry and worked on his own car. These areas of endeavor flourished under Howard's touch. The only jobs he didn't tackle were air conditioning and refrigeration.

If the problem wasn't readily apparent to Howard, his German tenacity kicked in. He refused to quit until he won. The malfunction was the adversary and Howard was the conquering hero. I cannot recall an instance when Howard gave up on a job as being too difficult or taking too long. His fledgling business, Rode's Repair, grew and Howard earned a reputation as an honest workman who did quality work for a reasonable price.

Samuel's birth approached. Being a back to nature type, my mom chose home births for my younger brother and sister. That family history coupled with several safe home births in our Christian fellowship gave me confidence to prepare to have Sam at home. A nurse friend, Susan, who was part of our fellowship, agreed to attend me.

A few days before Samuel was born the Lord impressed on my mind the scripture, "Let patience have her perfect work, that you may be perfect and entire, lacking in nothing," (James 1: 4, American Standard Version).

I clung to that scripture like a drowning man clings to a ring buoy as labor intensified and became painful beyond words. Susan had a vision. My soul's disavowal of children, inherited from generations past, had built an iron gate across my cervix. With every contraction a piece of the gate flew off. Knowing the pain advanced labor gave me the strength to endure. Eight hours later Samuel was born — all 8 lbs., 9 oz. of him. He was beautiful and despite the pain, I experienced a baptism of love.

The Bible describes this moment when new life emerges, "A woman, when she gives birth to a child, has grief because her time has come. But when she has delivered the child, she no longer remembers her pain because she is so glad that a child has been born into the world" (Jn. 16:21, Amplified Bible).

Truthfully, the pain was significant enough that I did remember it, but still, joy overwhelmed and encapsulated me. With wonder I gazed at Sam's every grimace, smile, and yawn. Howard and I rejoiced together. Our first-born child transcended our physical union and became a union of our lives, a portal by which we could go forward together.

I recalled Pastor Ben's exhortation three years previously, "God created you a woman and you will only be fulfilled as a woman." How true it was. We shared the news of Sam's birth with Ben and his new wife, Lydia. From the overflowing well in my inner being I expressed my joy, "Ben, I'm so happy."

"Oh, I can hear it in your voice."

In those first weeks after Sam was born, I wept often holding this precious life in my arms. I was overwhelmed by the goodness and mercy of God. My heart that was cold and empty toward children began to be filled with the love of God. *Began*, being the operative word as there was still much work to be done.

Daily life with Howard and a new baby settled into an easy predictability. Caring for Sam renewed my value to myself. I was a mother! Howard's new business prospered. He spent less time critiquing my deficiencies in housekeeping and more time focusing on his world of entrepreneurial excellence. Though we had arguments and ups and downs like all couples do, there was an increasing degree of communication, understanding, and compromise.

When Samuel was five months old, I watched him as he lay asleep and prayed, "God, I only have this one beautiful child in the garden of my life. May I have another?"

Within days I was pregnant. I laughed, "Lord, You answered that prayer a little faster than You do some of my other prayers!"

Howard declared, "If this child is a boy, his name will be Nathanael." Nine months later we did have another boy.

Because of my experience with Samuel's birth I presumed I was facing hours of intense pain and I was afraid. But labor was far easier and shorter, with strong contractions lasting a mere forty minutes and beautiful

Nathanael was born.

Again, I wept with joy, overcome that God would send such a priceless treasure to me. I reveled in my role as mother taking lavish care of our two sons, breastfeeding Nate, preparing organic, whole foods for Sam.

When Nate was a few months old he cried angrily for no reason. Jesus revealed the thought in his heart to me, *You don't love me. Mothers are supposed to love their children and you don't love me!*

I was horrified at this revelation. I was doing everything right at the natural level, yet I knew the indictment was true.

There was still a lot of cold emptiness in my heart and spirit. I felt so guilty. I was angry at myself and humiliated. *Every mother loves her children. What's the matter with me?*

In a still small voice God answered that thought by saying, *I am love, Karen. I'll give you love if you ask for it.* "Ask, and it shall be given you," (Mt. 7:7 King James Version).

Just embrace motherhood, right? That sounded simple enough. Just ask God to fill the void and make me whole. But to ask meant I would have to humble myself. I would have to admit I was broken and defective. I rebelled at admitting I was flawed in an area in which I thought everyone else was successful. At a prayer meeting with Ben and Lydia I choked out a confession of my failure as a mother.

Ben responded, "You have a difficult time giving a full expression of love to your children because you don't see them the way Jesus does." Then he looked at Howard.

"Howard, you do, don't you?" Howard nodded in agreement.

"Pray for Karen."

That was doubly humiliating and infuriating. Howard did nothing to care for our children. He never changed a diaper, never gave a bath, never dressed them, never fed them. I did all the work of attending to our two sons and Howard seemingly got all the credit for loving them. It was a terrible blow to my pride.

A few days later, praying through clenched teeth, I asked the Father for His love and His view of children. God hears prayer, even those squeezed out through offended pride. It was a prayer that would be answered a little at a time over the course of many years. On the cusp of this prayer, perhaps as an answer to it, I became pregnant with baby number three.

During this season two other doors blew open revealing hidden recesses of my heart that needed attention. These subconscious strongholds, these erroneous thoughts cemented together by strong emotion, became aroused and actionable in my life as a wife and mother.

The first door was discipline. One day, Howard removed the plastic cover of an old adding machine and laid it on the kitchen table so he could repair the faulty machine. Two-year-old Sam, cavorting around, knocked the cover to the floor and a piece broke off. Howard calmly reprimanded Sam and dispensed a few swats on his bottom.

"You must have been trained by the Gestapo!" I yelled.

Howard looked at me in bewilderment. My ludicrous reaction confused me as much as it did him. This event exposed a hitherto buried, irrational fear of discipline. Subconsciously, I equated discipline with punishment, even cruelty.

The second door opened into self-hate.

Housekeeping is not my first love or my top priority

in life and it became a soft target for Howard. His eye for perfection roamed the house, noticing my inconsistencies and mentioning them. Sometimes Howard's comments were justified and gave me the added push I needed to do the job. Sometimes his comments were nothing but nitpicking.

    Given my extreme, all or nothing personality, Howard's mild remarks became criminal indictments of my failure as a housemate. Occasionally, when these accusations built up in my head, self-hate boiled over into days of castigation. I punished myself by scrubbing the kitchen floor on my hands and knees or making extreme "to-do" lists that were impossible to complete. In my self-hatred I projected that scheduling every moment of my day with housework, thus penalizing my free spirit, would force me into the mold of what I thought Howard wanted in a wife.

    Of course, after running their course, those tirades of self-flagellation had to peter out into nothingness, and I was left unchanged. It would take years of work by the Holy Spirit to further expose and dismantle thought by thought, emotion by emotion, these fortresses built in my spirit.

    Most of the time, however, ordinary life filled my hours and days. Cooking and cleaning, laundry and dishes, caring for my babies and answering the phone for Howard's growing handyman business kept me busy. I loved my life. I biked through the neighborhood with Sam in a child seat behind me and Nate in a backpack on my back, took the boys to the local pet farm and read them stories. All the while my belly was growing large with another baby.

    A few days before I went into labor with our third child God gave me the scripture, "Arise, shine; for your light has come, And the glory of the Lord has risen upon you" (Isa. 60:1 New American Standard Bible).

With this being my third labor, I was confident I knew what to expect. But it was unlike the first two. Labor was so mild I thought, *This is going to take a long time.*

Whenever there was a little stronger contraction, the Lord said, "Affirm My program. I am good. Childbearing is good."

I whispered those affirmations and subsequent contractions were so mild as to be painless. At the moment of exit this baby came all the way out of my body in one long smooth contraction. Childbirth without pain; I wouldn't have believed it if it hadn't happened to me.

Choosing home birth in my day meant we didn't know the gender of the baby until the moment of birth. After two boys, we kind of expected another boy. It was a girl! We were overjoyed and named her Miriam.

Our family attended the regular Saturday night meetings of our small prayer fellowship. Together we pursued deliverance and cleansing, shared victories and burdens and prayed for one another. Pastor Ben traveled around the country teaching and praying for his flock, but his home base was California.

One of those ordinary gatherings proved to be extraordinary for me. Ben preached on the law of jealousy in Numbers 5 (KJV). The following day I re-read that chapter thinking, *I wonder if there is any more meaning to be found in these verses?*

Verse 28 rose out of the Bible in red capital letters and floated in front of my eyes as God's voice thundered in my mind, "AND SHE SHALL CONCEIVE SEED." I didn't know what to think. I had borne three children in two and a half years. Could God possibly be talking about another child so soon?

As had become a pattern to bring clarity to me in times of questioning, I had a vision. I stood on a plateau looking across a deep valley to another ridge. A group of beautiful children, like the Von Trapp family in *The Sound of Music*, skipped along the mountaintop, singing as they went.

Separated from those happy children stood a scrawny, malnourished child with big, sad eyes. He looked like the pictures you see of starving children in third world countries. His eyes spoke to me, *You wouldn't want me, would you.*

It wasn't a question. It was a statement. My heart went out to this forlorn looking child. "Yes, I do want you."

Instantly, he appeared on my side of the mountain, climbing the last remaining feet to where I stood, grinning from ear to ear. Weeks later I conceived child number four. I knew it was a boy. While still in the womb, we named him James.

With a growing family Howard and I looked for a larger home and more property. While my stomach grew for a fourth time, we purchased a newly built home on three acres on the outskirts of Fresno. We moved and Howard's handyman work kept him busy repairing water coolers, installing garbage disposals and dishwashers, and fixing plumbing leaks.

Months passed and the birth of our fourth child drew near. Since I recognized that generational influences had affected my own life and relationships, I could accept it when the Lord said to me one day, "Your baby's spirit is bruised."

God revealed in a mysterious way that forces in James' lineage included both being persecuted himself and persecuting others. Those spiritual dynamics not only impacted my birth experience with James but prompted us to intercede on James' behalf.

My understanding and experience of acting as an intercessor is as a go-between. An intercessor, yielding his vessel to the Holy Spirit, stands in the gap between God and the person in need. From that place of surrender the intercessor may feel the longings of God toward His child and/or enter into the sufferings of the individual needing prayer.

Probably my most dramatic experience of being used by God in this fashion was in one of Pastor Ben's prayer meetings in New York City. A young man was there from Guatemala. I had never seen him before and had no knowledge of his background. As we began to pray powerful emotion swept over me and I felt like I would die if this man, who I had never met, did not receive the help he needed from the Lord.

The Apostle Paul in Colossians 3:12 exhorts believers to "put on bowels of compassion and kindness."

I always thought that a strange expression until that prayer meeting. I literally felt that my bowels were falling out in compassion and yearning for this young man.

Intercession can take many forms. We learned in the ministry that fear and anger have physiological expressions. The body tends to be cold when fear arises; flushed with heat when anger is the predominant emotion. These negative emotions in concentrated form or combined with a weakened immune system can cause sickness.

This awareness gave a frame of reference for understanding the unusual events of James' birth. I believe it is possible to feel ill not from bacteria or viruses, but because either God is using you to intercede for others or spiritual forces within yourself are manifesting.

Intercession is a way of bearing one another's burdens (Gal. 6:2).

The time for James' birth arrived. Susan flew in from out of town to attend me. The day I went into labor, Susan woke up nauseated and continued feeling ill the entire day. That evening as labor intensified contractions became as painful as they had been with Sam. I was bewildered. After Miriam's painless birth experience, I expected repeat performances.

Have I made a wrong turn somewhere? This is not supposed to be happening.

Meanwhile, Howard also began feeling under the weather. The two people who were supposed to be aiding me languished on the floor barely functioning while I agonized in pain. Doubt and fear mounted in me as it seemed I was back to my first childbirth experience. Instead of caving to fear, we prayed.

In a few hours, James arrived safely. Physically, it was a normal delivery. Mentally and spiritually we were confused and questioning. The only explanation, I believe, is a generational one. God was calling us as parents in intercession to draw out a measure of fear, anger and doubt that wanted to embed itself into James' spirit. As we heard his first cries, there was the sense that God had won. Our fourth child had graciously been given a leg up in life. Beautiful, healthy James was welcomed into the family.

Seventeen-month-old Miriam expressed our joy perfectly. She toddled over to greet her brand-new, only hours old brother. One look and Miriam broke out into a jubilant dance, chortling and spinning in circles. Her ecstasy had to express itself in practical help. She ran to the couch, picked up diapers and blankets and piled them all around and on top of James who was lying on my lap. The excitement just could not be contained.

Every shared experience, such as interceding for James, built a bridge of communion and unity between Howard and me. Though he did not judge my natural skills worthy of an A+ rating, Howard was quite understanding and forgiving at the spiritual level. I could share my doubts, fears and troubles with him knowing I would receive safety and magnanimity from his heart.

Communication is essential to a happy marriage, but Jesus taught me a valuable lesson and built another bridge into my husband's heart when I stopped communicating.

At one of our meetings, Lydia taught that there are many types of fasts and God had recently led her to do a word fast. She stopped talking. Always up for a challenge that promised spiritual progress I began a three-day word fast. I spoke to the children when I needed to, but otherwise, I kept my mouth closed. That first evening Howard arrived home late from work. The children were already in bed.

I fixed Howard's supper, set his plate in front of him and started to walk away thinking, *Why sit down? I can't talk.*

But being nudged by the Spirit, I returned to the table. Howard chatted pleasantly about his day. Because I couldn't respond, I actually listened. It was amazing! I discovered nuances about my husband I hadn't noticed before — what he enjoyed about his work, what interactions he had had that day with his customers, the problems he had met and solved. I was fascinated--and all because I was compelled to really listen.

Chapter 5 | **The Redding Years**

Shortly after James was born, we sold our home in Fresno and moved to northern California. God provided an ideal house in Anderson, a small community just south of Redding. Sam turned five years old and I began homeschooling him. With my teaching degree it was natural for me to take charge of my children's education and include three other families in our fellowship. Two moms were single parents and needed to work so our home became both a school and a daycare center. With the help of a retired teacher friend, we had classes five days a week, calling ourselves, "The Lamb's School of Life."

    Occasionally Lydia visited and prayed with us bringing godly wisdom guiding us in this new venture. It was a wonderful season. The children were greatly enriched by having friends to play, pray, and learn with. Friendly competition spurred them on academically.

    They called each other at night challenging, "I'm going to do ten problems of math tonight."

"Well, I'm doing twenty!" And the race was on.

I learned the KISS principle--Keep It Simple, Stupid. When we first began our fledgling school, I wanted to run an elite academic program. I assigned the children the task of writing out the answers to the questions at the end of each chapter in their history books. They rebelled--squealing, complaining, refusing. After about a week of this total stand-off I took a step back to re-evaluate what I was doing wrong. I realized the children loved to read about history; they hated answering the questions.

I made an announcement, "No more answering the questions at the end of the chapters. Just read your history book." Whoops of joy greeted the news and peace descended.

That first lesson in the KISS principle became a guiding light throughout the remaining homeschooling years. If my efforts were met with an all-out pitched battle from my children, I would seek the Lord for a different approach. Ideas inspired by the Holy Spirit guaranteed cooperation from my children. . .usually.

I was the planner, organizer, decision maker handling the day-to-day schedule and studies for our home school venture. But when I reached an impasse--either with the dynamics of the children's interactions or a question on which direction to take next in the schooling process — I consulted Howard and he would join us in our morning prayer time. His presence and input would right the ship, bring godly wisdom and get us back on track spiritually. We could continue on several more weeks before another crisis arose.

It was always a blow to my pride to ask Howard for help. After all, I was the professional educator. I should be able to handle everything myself. God brought to my mind the rebellion of Korah in the wilderness. A group of

Israelites, with Korah as their spokesman, confronted Moses accusing him of taking too much authority unto himself.

That band of Israelites falsely accused Moses, but the indictment against me was true. I wanted to implement a successful educational program with happy, outstanding children all by myself. Then I could pirouette, exclaim, "Ta dah!" and sing with Frank Sinatra, "*I did it my way.*" So strong was my bent towards independence the lesson of interdependence would need repeating for years to come.

Once when Howard joined us in a morning prayer session one of the single moms jokingly asked him, "So, what do you think of marriage, Howard?"

We all expected the usual tomfoolery reply from my husband. Instead, he burst forth with, "Marriage is glory and honor and blessing. It's the glory of God manifest in the earth. . ."

Howard rhapsodized for several minutes about the splendors of marriage. We women were stunned into open-mouthed silence at this astonishing outpouring.

Teaching also came naturally to Howard. Being pressed upon by the children to build a tree house in the field in back of our house, Howard gathered the boys. He began by defining *plumb* and *level.* Later Howard quizzed these seven to ten-year-old future builders.

"What do we call a vertical line — 90 degrees from horizontal?" Howard asked as he drew an imaginary line in the air.

The boys hemmed and hawed, trying in vain to remember the word, until a light bulb went off in one energetic young man's brain. "Apricot!" he shouted. That wasn't quite the fruit Howard had in mind, but it was clear they were listening.

In February 1979 and July 1980, life became even

more bountiful with the arrivals of Sharon and Paul. Each pregnancy and unique birth experience enlarged my heart. Joy filled our home. Every baby was welcomed with gusto by the entire family with the exception of Paul. His birth precipitated alarm in one sibling.

Sharon was 17 months old when Paul made his entrance into the world. As the cute, adorable, sassy, youngest child Sharon had garnered many accolades. Even at her young age she wore the crown of princess confidently, assured that she could not be deposed.

The morning Paul was born Sharon toddled into the living room, took one look at her baby brother and threw herself on the floor in a full-fledged tantrum. A few moments later her better self came to the fore, and she conceded that, at least for now, she had been dethroned. Room must be made for the young prince. Sharon roused herself from the floor, came over and kissed Paul's cheek, which portended a continuing fond relationship.

Edith Ryan, one of the moms in our Christian fellowship, had trained vocally with coaches from Juilliard and performed in off-Broadway musicals. She was also a songwriter. Using my background in music I composed piano accompaniments for her songs. Three of us moms formed a trio and sang in church. These creative pursuits in music and writing that seemingly were buried when I married Howard rose in new life. I felt fulfilled.

Sometimes Howard's dominating personality coupled with his demands of perfection caused distress in both me and our children. But our shared joy in family, our unified goals in providing the best for our children, plus the busyness of life cushioned points of contention between us. We had found our stride.

Our bustling family life also helped blunt my thorns of self-hate and quiet the turmoil regarding discipline.

Sometimes I still fell into a slough of despond. On one of those occasions I was holding ten-month-old Paul shouting to Howard that God hated me because I was such a loser. My husband, his eyes pooled with grief, tried to reason with me. I refused his consolation, pushed past him and marched into the bathroom to change Paul's diaper. I laid my son down on the counter.

Looking into Paul's eyes they clearly communicated, "Oh, Mom, if you knew God the way I know God, you could never say that about Him." "A little child shall lead them" (Isa. 11:6 English Standard Version) the Bible says. I had refused my husband's help; I could not refuse my child's.

On the discipline front our children received a mixed bag. Though I no longer accused Howard of being trained by the Gestapo when he administered sane and just consequences for misbehavior, discipline was still a problem for me. In my mind discipline was synonymous with punishment. I could not bring myself to interrupt my children's happy lives with the downer of correction unless I became outraged at their behavior.

Though I knew discipline was necessary and I desired the benefits, I still hated it and only entered that domain when I was angry. Howard coddled his children when they were very young. As they grew older sometimes his actions spilled over into excessive control and criticism. My husband did possess a sense that I did not have--that work, even work that challenged you beyond what you thought you were capable of doing, built inner strength of character -- true grit. He modeled it himself and led his children in that way.

With six children, the oldest only seven-and-a-half-years-old, daily tasks overwhelmed me. I couldn't do it all and I had no outside help, no grandparents living close by to aid me. I repeatedly cried out in prayer to the Lord.

His answer was always the same, "Your helpers are in your own house." That was hard for me to accept. They were so young. Furthermore, I wanted to be able to do all the work myself. I considered my labor a gift of love to my family.

God had a different opinion. I often tell people the Lord sent an abundance of children to our home to save them from growing up incompetent in life skills. Fewer children would have made possible my skewed outpouring of love -- doing all the work myself. That was unachievable with that many little people to care for.

God strongly arrested me with this statement, "If you don't teach your children to work, you HATE them, you HATE them!" Why? Because they grow up weak-spirited, lacking not only in the natural skills necessary to build a successful life, but also lacking in the strength of will to achieve a prosperous existence.

I began by assigning Sam the job of bathing toddler James and getting him ready for bed each night. After a few days Sam confided to me, "I like taking care of James."

When James was five years old, he trudged into the kitchen to find me peeling pears to can. I was very discouraged looking at the mound of pears left to process. James asked, "Can I help?"

I sighed, "Oh, if only you could."

Just to make him happy I set him up with a pear and a peeler. He peeled the pear!

I ran outside and called to his older siblings, "Quick! I need help!"

With my four homegrown assistants I completed the impossible job of canning those pears, again proving God's dictum, "Your helpers are in your own house."

Sam was eight-years-old and growing fast. He rode his old used bicycle with his knees cocked to the sides because they no longer fit under the handlebars. Sam asked Howard to buy him a bike — a new one this time. Howard issued the terms — if Sam wanted a new bike he'd have to earn the money to buy it himself.

That challenge led to one of our most positive family experiences. Nate and Miriam, ages seven and six, decided they wanted to help their older brother. Their eagerness launched Rode's Bakery Service. Baking bread was natural to me. Following my mother's and grandmother's example, I supplied all of the family's bread requirements baking four loaves of bread every week. I also had my grandmother's famous recipes for cracked wheat dinner rolls and cinnamon buns. Rode's Bakery Service offered homemade bread, rolls and muffins. Sam made bread, Nate made rolls, Miriam made muffins. The trio walked the neighborhood selling their goods door to door.

Six weeks later the newly established bakery had earned $80. Howard took Sam to the store where he picked out a shiny, red bike. That evening the entire family gathered in the driveway. Everybody rode something — a bike, trike, or push toy. All the siblings trailed after Sam as he rode his new bike. Nate and Miriam were as delighted with Sam's new bike as if it was their own.

If one member be honored, all the members rejoice with it. (I Cor. 12:26 New King James Version). That summer evening, we experienced the best of what it means to be family.

Northern California boasts a rich and varied landscape which furnished our family with an assortment of experiences in nature. Mt. Shasta and Mt. Lassen an hour's drive away, north or south, provided snow for sledding in the winter. Lakes, streams and a neighbor's swimming pool insured swimming opportunities in the summer. And the blessings of God went far beyond the natural beauty around us as He rained down more babies — Joy and Lois in 1982 and 1983. Our crew of six turned into, seven and then eight.

One may ask, "Why, in this day and age, would you choose to have so many children?"

The seeds of that decision started in high school. Reading the account of Abraham, Isaac and Jacob, I was impressed by the diverse family structures of these patriarchs of Israel. Abraham and Sarah had one son, Isaac. Isaac and Rebekah had two sons, Jacob and Esau. Jacob, with his wives and their handmaidens, had twelve sons and many daughters. God doesn't have a one size fits all approach to families. Each situation is unique and has a purpose in God's design.

I wish I could trust God with family planning the way people did in Bible times. Too bad you can't do that these days.

When I discovered Pastor Ben endorsed trusting God with the number of children in a family, just like people in the Bible did, I rejoiced. Howard was on board with that idea before we met. The other believers in our fellowship supported young couples if they chose to believe God with family planning.

Shortly after Howard and I married, a mother of seven children shared, "With a large family every day there is something to laugh about, something to cry about, something to pray about. . ." That sounded like a wonderful life to me. I wanted it.

"Present your bodies a living sacrifice. ." the Bible exhorts (Rom. 12:1 KJV). I submitted myself before God and He allowed me the blessing of bearing many children.

Such a path is not for everyone, but it was the right path for me.

My commitment to God, however, did not exempt me from the ordinary frustrations of motherhood. Sam, Nate and Miriam were born 14 months apart from one another. Sam was two-and-a-half years old, barely out of diapers, when Miriam came along. I had Nate and Miriam in cloth diapers, never ending laundry, a nursing baby, a husband who had no frame of reference for childcare and no grandmothers close by to help.

But whether a person has one child or many, help or no help, life with kids is abundant in experience. There are tear-out-your-hair infuriating times and dance-in-the-streets joyful times sandwiched in between lots of just plain ordinary times. Every day brings a smattering of each reality. Because this life was His will for me, God gave me grace to do the job, poured an extra measure of joy over all and encouraged me when I was down.

In exasperation one day I exclaimed to the Lord, "Tell me again how wonderful it is to have children. I'm forgetting! I've tried Your program of fruitfulness, God, and I'm not feeling blessed today. In fact, I'm tempted to think You lied to me!"

The Father replied, "You've barely started down this path. How can you judge this journey with any credible authority until you've reached the end? You always wanted to go to heaven, and you think of children as balls and chains hindering your ascent. Why don't you see them as wings instead?"

It was true. I did have a lifelong ambition to go to heaven. My mother recounts that when I was three-years-old, in a fit of anger, I thrust my face into the dirt. She told me to stop because I would suffocate and die. I retorted, "I want to die and go be with Jesus!"

God answered my longing to go to heaven in a surprising way the fall of 1983.

Our church rented office space near Times Square, New York City and Pastor Ben invited families from prayer centers around the country to join him and Lydia. They planned to pass out literature on the streets of New York, pray outside the United Nations and have meetings at night. So as crazy as it may seem to travel with ten people, 3,000 miles across the nation, that's exactly what we did. Lois, child number eight, was two months old at the time.

Those were the days before mandatory car seats. Lois slept on my lap in the front seat of our Oldsmobile station wagon. Everyone else found a place in the back two seats. Most nights we slept in the car, putting the seats down in back so seven kids could sleep like sardines in a can.

In the days preceding our adventure, I felt this niggling by the Holy Spirit that He wanted to tell me something. I was too busy packing and preparing for the trip to take time to listen. One night, I took a turn driving while the rest of the family slept. I prayed, "Okay, Holy Spirit. Now I've got time. Just You and me and thousands of miles of road ahead. What were You trying to tell me?"

The Spirit brought to mind the scripture, "Suffer little children to come unto Me and forbid them not, for of such is the kingdom of God" (Lk. 18:16 KJV).

The words, *OF SUCH, OF SUCH, OF SUCH* reverberated over and over in my head. The Lord said, "You want to go to heaven. Children are the stuff, the "of such," the very fabric and composition of heaven. You're surrounded, inundated, flooded with the kingdom of heaven."

And so, I was--surrounded by Sam's old-for-his-age

maturity, Nate's gentleness, Miriam's spunkiness, James' crazy athletics, Sharon's china doll femininity, Paul's strength, Joy's zero-to-sixty temper, and Lois' newborn preciousness.

Howard's business, Rode's Repairs, continued to flourish. He purchased a large postal van secondhand and converted it to a traveling workshop. Everything needed for his jobs Howard carried in his truck. When his van lumbered into the driveway every evening all the children ran out to greet him, yelling, "Daddy, daddy, daddy" and threw themselves into his arms.

When Howard worked, he worked hard; when he played, he played just as hard, and quite often, silly. Each child as an infant and toddler enjoyed daily horsey rides on Howard's knee.

He swung them in the air as dads love to do, put their little feet on his big feet, held their hands and walked around the living room. He played a recording of German folk songs and danced around the house, stomping his feet and clapping wildly. When we all went roller skating a rink staff member waylaid Howard telling him to slow down because he was skating too fast and crazy. When Howard was in, he was all in.

Though I was a helicopter mom with regards to my children's spiritual life, I was laissez-faire in their natural life. And they loved it. Sam, Nate, Miriam and James roamed our semi-rural neighborhood amassing exploits worthy of Tom Sawyer. While I struggled to complete each day's tasks of cooking, cleaning, laundry and care of their younger siblings, they fished in ponds created by a gravel mine, explored the nearby "ghost town"-- an abandoned factory complete with buildings and tools -- and jumped off a rope swing into the Sacramento River.

Life was on cruise control. Howard's business

provided a comfortable living and Sam and Nate were learning entrepreneurship mowing neighbors' lawns and delivering newspapers. The younger six children were growing, healthy and happy. I cooked, baked, taught school, and sang with my friends. I wrote new school materials and designed and sewed a quilt and matching pillow sham for each of my children, artistically illustrating the meanings of each one's name.

    Family life had settled into a sweet ebb and flow. An unexpected phone call in the spring of 1985 would change all of that, bringing some of our family's greatest challenges and severest testings.

Chapter 6 | **The Mission**

Pastor Ben and Lydia were in New York City at our church's facility in Times Square. A man on the church's mailing list suggested they visit Divine Word Seminary, a former Catholic training facility for priests that was up for sale. Upon touring this school in upstate New York, Ben felt that our church should acquire this property. It's rural location in Conesus made it ideal as a prayer retreat. Our church discussed the merits of this faith venture and voted to proceed with the purchase.

     Ben phoned our home in California. Howard was at work, so I took the call. This new outreach for our church required a property manager and maintenance engineer. Did Howard want the position? Ben charged me with the task of presenting the proposal to Howard.

     The wheels of my imagination whirred. The patriarch, Abraham, had long been my hero. Upon hearing God's call, he risked everything and emigrated to a foreign country. Now I had the same opportunity to leave my extended family and West Coast culture behind and embark into the unknown. I envisioned this opportunity fulfilling all my desires -- living in a beautiful countryside place and accomplishing the "go-all-out-for-Jesus" requirements of giving up houses and lands and family for the sake of Christ. I would be in full-time Christian ministry, right in the middle of a new and exciting move of God. I knew Howard's perception would be very different from mine.

All jobs with our church were unpaid, volunteer positions. Howard had a wife and eight, soon to be nine, children to support as I was six months pregnant with our ninth child. Abandoning his successful business and moving 3,000 miles away to start over in an unknown venue would be an earthquake event for Howard registering a solid six or seven on the Richter scale. I looked forward to disturbing Howard's settled state with about as much excitement as I would have rousing a bear from hibernation. Truthfully, confronting the bear might be preferable, provided I had a ready escape.

When Howard walked in the door that evening, I pulled him into our bedroom to privately convey Ben's message. "Ben is looking for a maintenance man for the church's new property in New York. He wants to know if you would be interested in the job."

Howard reacted exactly the way I knew he would, "What?! Ben is off his rocker! What lamebrain idea has he concocted now! Craziest thing I ever heard of!" He marched out of our room and strode down the hall. In the time that it took Howard to walk that fifteen feet a change came over him -- something that can only be described as divine interruption.

All the children were in the living room. In completely uncharacteristic fashion Howard announced,

"You know what Ben wants us to do? He wants us to move to New York and live in a big facility the church just bought." The children started jumping around excitedly. Howard continued, "You mean you want to do something crazy like that?!"

Everyone laughed and yelled, "Yes, daddy, yes!" Howard laughed along with them and joy filled the house like water fills a swimming pool. In about sixty seconds time the decision had been made. No more discussion was needed. God had intervened, short-circuited Howard's apprehension and made clear the path of His will for our family.

Excitement filled those next months. Jonathan was born on June 12th. I was busy packing our entire household and caring for my ninth newborn. August 6, 1985, we exited our driveway with our Oldsmobile station wagon, a recently purchased 15 passenger van, both pulling trailers and Howard's work van, all packed to the roofs. Another family traveled to New York with us to attend meetings launching this new endeavor for our church. We wound our way across the United States in true caravan style.

The journey took seven days. In late afternoons it became the children's game to watch for billboards advertising KOA campgrounds in which to spend the night. Once we splurged and stayed in a motel with a water park. Considering the logistics of people and vehicles, our goal was to make the trip as timely as possible. Occasional stops at a park or a waterfall gave welcome respite.

In the final hours of our drive my mind scrolled through the rolodex of idyllic scenes painted by my imagination in the months preceding this move. All we knew was that this property was large and close to beautiful Hemlock Lake. I envisioned grass right outside our residence sloping gently to a sandy beach with beautiful pristine water for our children to swim in.

As we pulled up to the property, it was large and the water pristine — after that my imagination had totally failed me. We stepped out of the van and were surrounded by old and deteriorating buildings. Only the brick exteriors had escaped the ravages of time. Hemlock Lake was (and still is) preserved in its natural state because it is a water supply for nearby Rochester. My beach front vision was replaced with reality. Hemlock Lake was a quarter mile hike through woods down a very steep hill. The beach... non-existent.

But we did have plenty of room — a 110,000 square feet of classrooms and bedrooms and each bedroom had a private bath. Our children went from one bedroom for girls, one bedroom for boys, sleeping in bunk beds and sharing two bathrooms in California to two kids per room and bathrooms a plenty in New York.

The first challenge for Howard's job as maintenance man was water. Hemlock Lake was the sole water supply for the Mission. A pump at the lake forced water through underground pipes to a large water tank on the hill above the Mission. The water had to be judiciously chlorinated, the pump regulated, and the pipeline walked to check for leaks. Those first months Howard made daily trips down the hill to the pump house and up the hill to the water tank. He took Sam with him on these daily treks.

Shortly before we moved to New York Howard began complaining that his knees hurt. Years earlier, he had damaged them in a skiing accident and with age, the injury reasserted itself. The daily exercise of walking up and down steep hills healed Howard's knees. From that day forward, the pain never returned.

Over breakfast one morning I was flabbergasted to

hear Howard challenge Sam to a race from the pump house to the Mission after they completed their daily check-up. There were two paths to the lake -- the very steep shorter one which Sam chose and the longer, but less demanding one which Howard took. When I heard of the contest, I was certain 12-year-old Sam who had the height and strength of a 14-year-old would easily best 52-year-old Howard. I was wrong.

    Watching out the window of the Mission I saw Howard and Sam emerge from the woods surging the last hundred yards neck and neck. Only a photo of the finish could have determined the winner. It was declared a tie. I thought the race an incredible display of showmanship, especially on Howard's part. It certainly proved the extent of his healing.

    After the water supply was secured, reliable heating and plumbing were next on the maintenance agenda. Howard's handyman abilities were challenged a thousand per cent. He had never seen a steam heat system. Now he was faced with two boilers, one of them an old behemoth twenty feet long that needed servicing. It was in better shape than the other boiler which virtually needed resurrection from the dead. Fortuitously, there was a local man Howard met who knew where to find parts for these outdated contraptions and worked days and weeks with Howard to bring them into working order.

    While adults and older children worked the younger children cavorted in paradise. What could be better than exploring a ginormous old building from basement to attic? There were treasures to be discovered, passageways to be explored, and that was just one building. There were garages, the former cattle barn, the pavilion, the burn pit, the dump on the hill. Huck Finn would have drooled with envy at the 40 acres of woods with a secluded pond replete with frogs, dragonflies and other water creatures.

Years previous the Catholics had created a picturesque park in the dip of land adjoining the seminary. They called it the Grotto. Two caves displayed statues depicting scenes surrounding the birth and death of Jesus. In addition, there were several stations honoring saints scattered throughout the park.

A stream bisected the Grotto and ran under the road. Following the stream towards Hemlock Lake the lay of the land formed a natural eight-foot water slide over shale. Our children ripped the seat out of many a pair of shorts and bruised their bottoms slipping and sliding down the shale, but oh, the fun.

The thrill was not only in body surfing the water slide, but also getting to it. There were two ways to access the slide. One was through the tunnel under the road, the other was down the nearly perpendicular hill in the forest. They faced claustrophobia in the tunnel and the possibility of a painful fall and tumble over rocks and tree roots on the hill. Either way added that dab of danger to bring the whole adventure to exhilarating heights.

That winter Murphy's Law applied -- whatever could go wrong in that old seminary, did go wrong. Every day brought new challenges. A water pump failed and had to be replaced. The boilers required constant attention. The chlorine content of the water had to be closely monitored.

Our lives revolved around the weather. We came to appreciate frigid temperatures that kept snow and ice frozen and dreaded the periodic thaws which revealed areas of the roof that leaked like a sieve.

I always said Howard brought the precision mentality of a German watchmaker to every task. His propensity toward the meticulous was overwhelmed with the needs of this huge, old building. Solving the heating and plumbing problems consumed his thoughts and time. He began to work 12-15 hour days refusing to take time out even to eat. I brought his meals to wherever he was in the building so he could eat with one hand and keep a tool in the other.

Sam, being the oldest, became Howard's number one assistant, supplemented by 11- year-old Nate. Other young teens from families in our fellowship who lived at the Mission for various lengths of time, added to the workforce. Once this crew had to pull an all-nighter monitoring the boiler. I turned it into a pizza party for the boys to make their vigil easier.

Working with Howard was not something looked forward to by these young men. The days were long and boring as Howard's impulse to control everything prevented the boys from doing any of the actual work. They were consigned to standing around and handing Howard the tools he requested. But these lads did learn patience, a good work ethic, and above all, to clean up after one's self.

One of the joys of being at a location with such a rich history was the people who stopped by and told us stories of their association to the Mission. We heard it over and over, "Being here is my fondest childhood memory."

At its peak in the 1950's the Catholic church owned four hundred acres surrounding the Mission. The property was dedicated to preparing young men for the mission field and priests from Divine Word Seminary were sent all over the world. The seminary was completely self-sufficient with its own winery, wheat fields, animal barn, slaughter house, even shoe making equipment. When enrollment for the priesthood declined and the seminary closed, Livonia School System rented classroom space for their fifth and sixth grade students while their new building was under construction. The children privileged to attend school at the Mission declared it to be their best years.

Those first months at the Mission we lived the scripture, "But if we have enough food and clothing, we will be content with that" (1 Tim. 6:8 NIV).

Food and clothing were all we had. Like Elijah in the wilderness ravens fed us. The ravens came in the form of the Miller Brothers nursery. A truck showed up unannounced and unloaded box after box of apples, along with onions and potatoes.

We heard the story that these brothers as youngsters attended fairs put on by the Catholic diocese in the open field opposite the seminary. The boys rode with their parents in a horse drawn buckboard to these fairs. The Millers had fond memories of those days and heard that our church had purchased the property. Ideal weather conditions that summer produced a bumper crop of apples, too many for them to sell, and they thought of us. Although we were strangers the Millers' attachment to the Mission stirred them to action. Boxes of produce lined the basement walls, providing sustenance all winter. It was a humble, yet beautiful beginning.

Sam, Nate and Miriam learned to bake apple pies with this "manna from heaven." That winter they each made themselves an apple pie for lunch every day. Matsu apples were a new variety of apple and they were huge. Three apples filled a pie pan. To this day, Nate holds the title, "Premier Apple Pie Baker." Whether it's determining the extra smidgen of oil or water needed for the perfect pie crust, or his preparation of the apples with just the right amount of sugar and cinnamon, Nate's record remains unchallenged.

One of our most love-filled, joyous experiences occurred the year after we purchased the Mission. It was

December. Five other families were temporary residents and we were all in strained financial circumstances.

As the leader of our cooperative home school, I pondered, *How can I make Christmas "Christmas" for all of us?*

I recalled a childhood incident. Twice my family had played "Secret Santa" to friends and neighbors. We owned a Santa suit with a full-face mask. My Mom purchased humorous items meaningful to the recipients and wrote a jingle to accompany each gift. On Christmas Eve my Dad donned the Santa suit and we drove stealthily to the neighbors' homes, turning off the car lights the final 500 feet to the house.

Ringing the doorbell, my Dad "ho-hoed" his way into their living rooms, read the poems, handed out the gifts, then ran back to the car where my Mom prepared for a fast getaway. It took weeks of sleuthing before our bewildered neighbors uncovered the identity of Santa. It was great fun.

That memory became a template for action to solve the dilemma of Christmas at the Mission that year. The children were assigned angel duty. We put the names of every adult in a bowl and the children drew a name. Each child was commissioned to act as a secret angel to the person whose name they drew. In addition to our regular studies we spent the month of December making crafts and planning surprises.

Love and joy filled our days as we anticipated the responses of the adults to our Christmas offerings. We especially looked forward to the squeals and hugs from the older women in residence who had no relatives close by with whom to celebrate Christmas.

Borrowing from the theme of the twelve days of Christmas we planned the Seven Days of Christmas. The children would surprise his or her secret person with a gift every day the week before Christmas and reveal their identities at the Christmas Day banquet. The first gift was an angel made out of poster board and decorated with glitter. An attached poem announced, "You have a secret angel preparing blessings for you."

On the days that followed, small stockings were sewn out of scraps of material and filled with candy. The children then decorated bags to be filled with popcorn. And other crafts were handmade for each recipient. Each day the children delivered their gifts to each person's door as we walked through the halls singing carols.

A writing assignment for English class became one of our presents. The task was to create a card and write a poem for the special person. The card I helped Nate create for his secret angel target, Margaret, we thought perfect.

Margaret was in her 60's and had taken it upon herself to paint the walls of this old building. Every day she was up on ladders, sloshing paint. Using construction paper Nate fashioned a large paintbrush and I helped him write a humorous poem to go inside--something about eternal job security since the Mission walls seemed endless.

On the designated day, each child put their card in his/her person's mail slot. Nate and I couldn't wait to see Margaret's reaction, so we called, "Oh, Margaret, you have mail."

Margaret came into the mail room, pulled out her card and began reading it out loud. She hooted, she howled, she slapped her knees and stomped her feet in uproarious laughter after every line. There could be no greater reward for our efforts.

Christmas Day was the grand finale. We ate turkey dinner and the children revealed their identities as secret angels and received grateful hugs from the adults. None of us had financial wealth that December, but the riches of love and laughter made it one of the best Christmases ever. The spirit of the season engulfed everyone, and 30 years later, secret angels are alive and well. It is now a cherished family tradition.

Ringing in a new year, it was becoming clearer than ever that my ambition to engage in full-time Christian service, was being satisfied. Caring for a husband and nine children was definitely full time. Moving to the Mission was the ultimate dream come true for my spiritual self. My never-ending mountain of tasks and my striving after holiness had secured a place for me on the cutting edge of this exciting move of God and I was bringing my family with me to these spiritual heights. I was exultant.

Though the physical challenges were many and our financial constraints severe, the bubble I created of imagined spiritual success sustained me. Still clinging to the image of ethereal perfection I felt that here, in this situation, I would finally acquire spiritual acclaim and bask at ease in my new, shinier holiness.

The strength of my desire was unquenchable. It manifested in mixed motives and skewed desires for my children. I wanted them to be strong in the Lord and serve Him with all their hearts, but my ambition was not just for their good, but also for my image. Their excellence would enhance and bring credibility to the belief that I was a super spiritual woman of God.

I pressured my children with unwanted exhortation, always backed up by scriptures and delivered with the fervor of an evangelist. If I felt I had failed in my attempt to make Howard or our children act spiritually pure, I became depressed, and in a desperation befitting a life and death crisis, I would try even harder. Though I was earnestly and sincerely pursuing the things of God, I was also pursuing personal aggrandizement and worship for self.

God began to stand against this rogue disease in my soul. Instead of receiving accolades from Lydia and my prayer warrior friends and colleagues I began receiving the "sharper than any two-edged sword, ... and judging the very thoughts and purposes of the heart" (Heb. 4:12 AMP).

I became distraught. Despair expelled hope. I continuously failed to meet Howard's standard of perfection in the natural. That same sense of inadequacy bled into my spiritual life. The Brillo pad of the Holy Spirit scoured my heart and the shiny veneer of holiness I had so carefully overlaid on my life by good works began to tarnish.

One evening I fell into the blackest of self-recrimination. I compared myself with people I admired. Acknowledging their hard work and accomplishments, I judged myself fatally and hopelessly flawed. I reached a dead end. I convinced myself that God's "I love yous," in the Bible were written for everyone but me.

"I love you," a line that would make almost anyone feel important and cared for, morphed into a mockery. God said, "I love you."

I heard, "I wish I could love you but you're not good enough."

Living in a 110,000 square foot building provides innumerable niches in which to hide. So, I left my children and husband upstairs and made my way down to a basement corner of the Mission. I sat in the darkness of my self-condemnation and battered my body, slapping myself in the face and punching my arms and legs repeatedly. Welcome to the prison of my self-hate.

Chapter 7 | **Out from The Ashes**

"Where can I go from Your Spirit? Or where can I flee from Your presence? If I ascend to heaven, You are there; if I make my bed in hell, behold, You are there" (Ps. 139:7,8 New American Standard Bible)

I made my bed in hell that night in the farthest corner of the basement and I soon discovered, like King David, God was there. I wasn't met with rays of glorious light or a quick solution, but in that lonely place I knew He was there with me.

After sitting alone in the dark, I climbed the stairs and slipped into bed unnoticed. In the middle of the night, after falling into an exhausted sleep, I woke up abruptly. I felt the tangible breath of God over my mouth and nose. Earlier that day I read a story of a man camping in the wilderness who came across newborn beaver kits, knowing the mother was dead. He held each kit to his face and breathed into its mouth and nose, "willing the kit to live." God was willing me to live.

But living isn't always easy. In the days and weeks that followed I awoke saying, "God, I can't do this. I can't function." Each time God replied, "You have to for Jonathan's sake." Jonathan was five months old at the time and God knew the strongest motivation to stir me to life was caring for the one who needed me the most -- my baby.

I struggled internally for months. Simultaneously, the physical workload increased as well. Our family's residence in the main building of the Mission had from the beginning been considered temporary. The former nun's house on the knoll overlooking the seminary was to be our home. When the school was fully functional with 400 priests in attendance, eight nuns drawn first from Italy, then Austria, cooked and did laundry for the young men. They lived in the Shaker style brick house with four rooms on the first floor, eight tiny bedrooms on the second floor and a basement full of laundry tubs and mangle irons. There was a bath and a half and no kitchen as the nuns cooked and ate at the Mission.

Visitors told us the nuns kept their house so immaculate you could eat off the floors. With the decline of candidates for the priesthood, the house had other tenants who, obviously, did not share in the nun's obsession for cleanliness. We were met with cracked plaster walls, rooms painted half chocolate brown, half chartreuse, and a dead raccoon in the attic. This real-life situation became a training ground for Nate and Sam. They were mere lads, 13 and 14 years old. Renovating the nun's house required them to work like men.

Howard was unfamiliar with plaster walls. He tried

to use conventional methods to repair the holes, filling the fissures with mud. The mud cracked. Howard dug out the mud and re-did it, teaching his sons the fine art of mudding. Over and over the process was repeated. Eight hours a day for two straight months Sam and Nate worked on the walls in the living room. Finally, Howard tried filling the deeper cracks with wood putty first, letting it dry, then overlaying it with mud. That proved successful.

    Desperate to make progress in renovating the house that had proved to be so frustrating, Howard asked me to help. Again, and again he patiently showed me how to apply mud to the baseboards and walls. Howard put the mud on so skillfully it needed only the lightest touch up of sanding afterwards. My attempts to ace "Mudding 101" produced C+ results. In my already distressed state of mind, the task of mudding baseboards piled up more damning evidence that I was failing on every front.

    Sam and Nate, however, became experts in both mudding and painting. To satisfy Howard's above and beyond the call of duty requirements, the boys painted the walls five and six times. So skilled were they Howard delegated the interior paint job of a small office in Livonia to the Sam and Nate. The boys did the work with professional excellence far beyond their years.

    The work at the nun's house seemed endless and the training relentless. Sam and Nate worked with Howard to install a wood stove. An on-demand hot water heater and a complete kitchen soon followed. Being the eldest, Sam bore the brunt of Howard's on-the-job instruction. With long hours and harsh demands, Sam began to despise his dad and to hate work. It is to Sam's credit that at his young age he overcame his hate for his dad and work, setting an example and a standard for his siblings to follow.

    To this day I believe Howard's greatest gift to our

children was an exceptional work ethic. They learned how to work and work hard. They learned what it means to be diligent, persevere, and sweat until the job is done right. Our children earned a reputation in the community, as their father had, for quality service. It was known that if you hired a Rode, he or she would perform the task, large or small, with excellence.

Taking a rare break from the drudgery of working on the house, Howard and I celebrated our April birthdays at a local restaurant. Howard told me to order anything I wanted. I couldn't believe he was being so kind as to pay for a meal at a restaurant. We had so little money and I felt I didn't deserve the lavishness that a restaurant meal represented. Howard's small act of kindness was a golden thread of the love of God--a lifeline reaching out to me in my darkness.

What ultimately pulled me out of that mental and emotional pit was the Word, specifically the words of Jesus. "The words that I speak unto you, they are spirit and they are life" (John 6:63 KJV).

My pastors taught that every word Jesus spoke has the seed of life within it. Our church published a red-letter manual with only the words of Jesus from Matthew to Revelation.

I thought, *I don't know anyone who needs life more than I do right now. I'm going to try it.*

Over the next couple of weeks, I read the red-letter manual three times. Each time I felt like I was being pulled up into newness of life. At the end of the third time the life flowing into my heart, mind, and spirit, was so miraculous that the thought burst forth, *Little children MUST have this life available to them!*

I soon started to write a book and illustrate the words of Jesus for children. Beginning with Matthew 3:15,

I drew a picture to convey the meaning of each scripture so that the smallest child could comprehend the love of Jesus.

I had nine children to feed, sew clothes for and homeschool. The only time available to work on this project was the early morning hours. Six days a week I arose at 5:00 a.m. and worked until 7:00 a.m. I produced two illustrations per day until I had completed all of Matthew chapters 3-7. There were days I didn't want to get up. It was winter and the room I used for art had no heat, but I was committed to this undertaking. The reward of seeing the words of Jesus come to life pulled me out of bed every morning.

The day I illustrated Matthew 6:33, "Seek ye first the kingdom of God, and his righteousness; and all these things shall be added unto you," brought special blessing.

I woke up that morning feeling particularly low. How could I create a visual representation of that scripture? Then the breakthrough happened. I drew a castle representing the Kingdom of God with two children facing the gate. Then I began to list all these things added in the air around the children that they had access to: love, joy, peace, patience, kindness, food, clothes, blessing. I filled the page with add-ons and by the time I finished my spirit was soaring on thermals of joy and thanksgiving! With every completed page the experience of fulfillment and life was a tangible one.

I called my book, *The Yum-Yum Tree*. The name was taken from scriptures in Revelation 22:14, "Blessed are they that do his commandments, that they may have right to the tree of life, and may enter in through the gates into the city;" and in John 6:57, "... He that eats Me shall live by Me."

After two years living in the large expanse of the Mission, our family moved into our home on the hill.

Several circumstances lifted our family to a plateau where life, again, became settled and easier. The emergency maintenance details of the Mission had been resolved and another man took over the day to day needs of that facility. Howard had transferred his entrepreneurial skills from general handyman in California to heating and plumbing expert in New York. His new business, A & O Services, was born and thrived.

My work seemed never ending and I was easily overwhelmed at times. Exhortations, whether they came straight from the Lord or through people, strengthened me to do what God was asking of me.

One afternoon as I walked up the hill from the Mission towards our house, I was feeling discouraged and defeated. I saw in the spirit God grab my shoulders, fling me back and forth urging, "You've got to pull yourself together, you're going to have another baby."

Well, for that reason and that reason alone, I'll try to pull my life together. Shortly after, I was with child… for the TENTH time.

Nine months later Susanna was born. It had been three years since we had welcomed a baby into our home, the longest span between any of our children. Susanna's siblings fought each other for holding rights. Those first weeks of life she was in someone's arms continuously.

With her blond hair and Shirley Temple curls, Susanna became the darling of the family. Her devastating cuteness saved her from being pummeled by her siblings when she woke them up in the morning.

Two-year-old Susanna functioned as a human alarm clock. I sent her upstairs in the mornings and she gleefully raced from one sibling to the next, bringing her tiny fist down on whatever body part she could reach commanding, "Wake up!" WHAM! "Wake up" WHAM! Downstairs in the kitchen, I chuckled hearing her run from bedroom to bedroom. It was wonderful.

We had five boys and five girls, a balanced family with perfect bookends — blond, blue-eyed Susanna the picture-perfect ending to brown haired, brown-eyed Sam, the joy-filled beginning of the family.

One day I happened on an article in Reader's Digest about a family of six children who had decided six was enough and were in shock when several years later mom became pregnant with number seven. The mother shared how it was difficult to look forward with joy to this unexpected event. But this surprise daughter turned out to be a special spirit who brought buckets full of blessing, happiness, peace and goodwill to the family. She was the bonus child they didn't know they needed.

Being the type of person who wants to be sure I have not missed out on anything, I began to pray, actually beg God, for a bonus baby of my own.

Chapter 8 | **Growing Pains**

God answered my prayer and at age 42 I was pregnant with our eleventh child. All my pregnancies had been problem-free, and the pattern held true for this pregnancy except for excessive weariness. I was so tired I began eating meals in bed. My go-to mode of relaxation is reading but much of the time I was even too exhausted to read. I just stared at the walls.

On June 15, 1990, we welcomed Rachelle into our family. She weighed 5 pounds 12 ounces, the smallest of our children. Although I had carried Rachelle full term, she looked and acted premature. Those first few weeks she vomited much of my breast milk and lost a pound. I feared for her life. The downward trend reversed, however. She began digesting milk and slowly gained weight. Seven months and many bowls of oatmeal later Rachelle caught up to the size and weight of a normal, healthy child.

Planning meals and cooking for a family of 13 meant I never left the kitchen. By the time I cleaned up after one meal, it was time to prepare for the next. My teenagers, my most competent helpers, had full-time jobs of their own that left little time to help out at home. Our Heavenly Father, ever mindful, ever efficiently solving, aiding, making progress in everyone's circumstance, intervened.

A few months after Rachelle was born the temporary residents at the Mission left for the winter, leaving just our family to tend to the property. Pastor Ben asked 17-year-old Sam, along with Nate and James, to take the leadership role of being caretakers for the main building. Of course, the boys had Howard's experience as back-up in shouldering this large responsibility. Sam, Nate and James moved out of our family home, into the Mission, and officially into adulthood. Sam's and Nate's jobs provided some of their financial needs.

At first Sam and Nate shared groceries and meals. Then skinny, 5'11" Nate began to notice that 6'4" Sam ate a whole lot more than he did, but he was paying for half of the groceries. Nate rebelled at this inequity and the two bachelors each began buying their own groceries and cooking for themselves. It was both amusing and heartwarming for me to observe the boys sort out their living arrangements.

It was mostly due to Howard's efforts that our sons were prepared for this challenge in life. His training program, though faulty, built strong and independent people, unafraid of facing life head-on with all its trials. The move proved a dual blessing. Our sons grew in body, mind and character with the umbrella of Howard's and my presence and support a stone's throw away. And I was relieved of cooking for 13 people, giving me much needed time and space.

Age 15 was a tough year for James. He had utter and complete confidence that he was qualified to run the show

— everybody's show. He upbraided Howard and me, telling us we had grown soft in our old age and weren't disciplining his younger siblings properly. He stepped on Joy's and Lois' toes because he thought they should wear shoes while they delighted in being barefoot all summer. I had to repeatedly tell James, "Your Dad and I are raising your siblings exactly the way we raised you. We've got this. If we need your help, we'll let you know."

James observed Sam and Nate living independently and making all their own decisions. It looked like wondrous freedom to him. He was so anxious to be on his own with nobody telling him what to do. He hired on at a local horse farm.

I worried about James, and God gave me a vision. I saw a large eagle's nest high up on a mountain ledge. The nest, full of eaglets, represented our family. Howard, the full-grown eagle, soared around, engaged and intent in his protector/provider role. Sam, the teenager, was testing his wings, exploring the thermal air currents close to the nest. James was hanging on the side of the nest, flapping his not quite ready wings furiously.

Sometimes he lost his balance and swung under the edge of the nest, talons gripping the side as he exclaimed, "Whoa!" And God quieted my heart with, "Be anxious for nothing. I am fully aware and present in your situation and I can handle James."

Working at the horse farm adjusted James' attitude. Mucking out stalls, interacting with surly fellow employees, being tossed about by half-broken racehorses, and paying all his own bills compelled James to admit, "Being on my own is harder than I thought it would be." Life is tough. Reality tends to knock off our rough edges and prove our mettle.

A few days after Sam turned 18, Howard informed

him that he was now an adult and on his own financially. Howard made this proclamation without my knowledge. When I found out I was shocked, and I was afraid for Sam.

The Lord calmed me with, "Fear not, this is of Me." And it was. The next day one of Howard's heating customers called asking Howard if he knew anyone he could employ to remodel his house. Without hesitation, Howard recommended Sam.

That initial job not only provided Sam with food, gas money and valuable work experience but also mushroomed into work for years to come. The man and his extended family became lifelong friends and clients of Sam's fledgling construction business and recommended him to everyone they knew.

Entrepreneurship requires filing government forms. That first year of business Sam tackled filling out an IRS form. He strode into the house, waving the paper, plopped himself down on the couch calling, "Dad, sit right down here beside me. I've filled this out and I just have one question."

Howard refused, responding, "You're smarter than I am, Sam, figure it out for yourself," and left the room.

Again, I was horrified. Later, when I questioned Howard, he made this astonishing statement.

"If I help Sam, he doesn't get strong. If he struggles and figures it out for himself, he'll never forget that piece of information."

Personally, I felt the father-son bond needed strengthening at that point in time. In my judgment enjoying each other's company while filling out an IRS form should have taken precedence over pushing Sam further away into independence.

Therein lies the delicate balance and challenge of parenting. Training a child to persevere through challenges and develop a hardiness of spirit is valuable to a child. Saddling children with tasks so burdensome that it fosters dejection and discouragement produces weak and timid souls. John Locke, a 17th-century British philosopher, states such overburdened children "very seldom attain to anything."

Mr. Locke further contends, "He who knows how to reconcile these seeming contradictions has, in my opinion, got the true secret of education."[2]

Two aspects of Howard's character, perfectionism, and control, both blessed and cursed us. He was the undisputed head of our family. I rejoiced that he was strong and unyielding when the young bucks, our teenage sons, challenged him. And his performance on his jobs was sterling. Proudly, honestly, I promised potential customers, "My husband can solve your heating or plumbing problem -- guaranteed."

But Howard loved ruling too much. When our sons and daughters reacted to his demands for perfection with understandable, age-appropriate immaturity, Howard castigated them as rebels against his authority. Excellent workmanship is a worthy attainment and a benefit to society. Howard believed this end justified his means. More and more I grieved believing that our children were experiencing too much law and not enough love from their father.

The axiom of "when one is honored, all members rejoice," brought revisited blessings to our family. Sam and Nate were looking for steady work in the field of construction, while Miriam had begun working as a mother's helper for a woman named Diana. Miriam was a dream come true for her employer. Being trained in Howard's school of work, she was available on a moment's notice and did everything asked of her from scrubbing floors on her hands and knees to teaching Diana's two preschoolers to write.

Miriam told Diana that her brothers wanted to work in the construction field. Diana replied, "I know the owner of DeMarco Construction, the premier builder in this area. I'll recommend your brothers to Roger, sight unseen, because of what I know of you."

Diana did recommend Sam and Nate to Roger and he hired both boys. When James turned 18, DeMarco Construction also hired him which resulted in many successful years of employment for all three brothers. Sam continued to expand his own construction business evenings and Saturdays.

As our older children matured to young adults Rachelle grew to be cute as a button. When she smiled her whole face crinkled up and her eyes disappeared into slits. She loved music and wore out the *Wee Sing Bible Songs* cassette tape that she could operate herself in her Fischer Price cassette player. When she was three years old Rachelle was often mysteriously missing from the hubbub of whatever her siblings were doing. Invariably, a search discovered her upstairs on her bedroom floor listening to Bible songs.

Rachelle delighted us with her Amelia Bedelia perception of life. Taking statements literally and acting on them, she splashed our daily lives with the freshness of a different perspective. When the tea kettle whistled and dripped water droplets Rachelle compassionately observed, "Mommy, the tea kettle is crying."

As parents sometimes tend to do, I ignored or explained away signs that perhaps all was not right with Rachelle. She was a few months delayed in crawling and walking.

She's fine. She'll catch up. Nothing to worry about.

When Rachelle was five years old and enrolled in the Kindergarten class at our home school co-op organization, her teacher pointed out to me that the figures of people Rachelle drew with enlarged eyes and misplaced arms and legs indicated a problem.

I'll just work harder with her.

I drilled Rachelle in phonics and math concepts, but her mind was a sieve. All information fell through the holes and the next day found me teaching the same material again. When summer temperatures reached the nineties, Rachelle wore three or four skirts on top of one another as if she couldn't feel the heat. We ran the gamut of doctors, nutritionists, and programs with little effect. I kept plugging along teaching the same school lessons day after day hoping for a breakthrough.

My ten children had pushed, pulled, and jostled me on the way of love. Rachelle was to carve out a new path, one that I thought I could never tread. Having a child who pulled on all my resources daily caused me to stumble and fall on this new journey. Through the years I had observed mothers of special needs children be miracle workers in their children's lives.

Will I ever be a good enough mother to care for a child who needs so much from me? I don't think I can do this. I don't think I can be good enough.

I was afraid. I was resentful. Although performing the required outward duties, spiritually I held myself somewhat aloof. It took years and tears to commit to a fuller expression of motherhood for Rachelle.

Around this time God returned to another of my fears. One Saturday morning the Spirit instructed me to do a Bible word study on "discipline." Dismay rose up in my heart and mind.

There was that dreaded word again. I'm afraid to

find out what the Bible has to say. I'll feel condemned because of my neglect to implement proper discipline with my children.

The only verse in the Bible translated *discipline* in the King James version is found in Job 36:10. "He opens their ear to discipline and commands that they return from iniquity."

So far, so good. Opening the ear to discipline I can go along with.

Then I discovered the word translated *sound* in 2 Timothy 1:7 (KJV) could also be translated *disciplined*, as in "For God has not given us a spirit of fear; but of power, and of love, and of a sound (disciplined) mind."

I researched every word associated with discipline in the Hebrew, Greek and English dictionaries. *Chasten, instruct, correct, reprove, doctrine, save, protect, train* are embodied in the concept of discipline, which reminded me of 2 Timothy 3:16. "All scripture is given by inspiration of God and is profitable for doctrine, for reproof, for correction, for instruction in righteousness."

Amazing! That verse could just as well be translated, "All scripture is given by inspiration of God and is profitable for discipline, for discipline, for discipline, for discipline." To what purpose? "So that the man of God may be complete and proficient, well fitted and thoroughly equipped for every good work" (2 Timothy 3:17 AMP).

My mind was largely transformed by the word of God that Saturday morning. Nevertheless, it would still be years before the teaching that I believed with my mind would be fully realized in my day to day life. To my heart discipline still equaled punishment. I held it an unpleasant task to be avoided if at all possible and only implemented as a last resort.

In pursuit of better understanding, I acquired Michael Pearl's book, *To Train Up a Child*. It both horrified and challenged me. Michael actually enjoyed training his children in the fine art of self-discipline. He deliberately created situations and games to encourage character development. I couldn't imagine! What I judged distasteful, he loved. While I admired Michael's ability and success, I could not follow his advice. Discipline remained a dreaded word and concept. I tucked his book away and continued my inconsistent, "only when angry" disciplinary patterns with my children.

Truthfully, the anger was becoming quite consistent. I was angry a lot. In fact, I was tearing my hair out. The endless squabbles among the younger children all day, every day, especially about work, made my life miserable.

In a large family, delegating work responsibilities is not an option; it's a matter of survival. I spent time making master lists of chores for each child and set up teams. On paper, it looked good. But then you have real, live kids to deal with who 1) don't want to work, 2) are certain their siblings aren't required to do as much as they are 3) enjoy fighting and 4) resent receiving instruction from any other sibling. I had an organization composed of all bosses, no underlings. I couldn't take it anymore. But God is faithful. Whenever I had reached the end with my children and cried out in desperate need God answered, helping me grow just a little bit more.

An idea came to me that was so brilliant, I knew it could only have come from God. Since everyone wanted to be chief and tell everyone else what to do, we began a study of what qualities the Bible says are required of a shepherd, bishop, elder. From 1 Timothy 3 and 1 Peter 5, we made a list and studied one character trait per day in our morning Bible and prayer time. A leader, according to

Scripture, must be "circumspect and temperate and self-controlled; [he must be] sensible and well-behaved and dignified and lead an orderly (disciplined) life; [he must be] hospitable and be a capable and qualified teacher, not given to wine, not combative but gentle and considerate, not quarrelsome, but forbearing and peaceable" (1 Tim. 3:2-3, AMP).

And from 1 Peter 5:1-3 (AMP), "I warn and counsel the elders among you. . .Tend (nurture, guard, guide, and fold) the flock of God that is [your responsibility], not by coercion or constraint, but willingly; not dishonorably motivated by the advantages and profits [belonging to the office], but eagerly and cheerfully; Not domineering [as arrogant, dictatorial and overbearing persons] over those in your charge, but being examples (patterns and models of Christian living) to the flock."

That's a very thorough list. It took weeks to examine all the qualifications required to be the one in charge. Then we read John 10:27, "My sheep hear My voice, and I know them, and they follow Me" (Holman Christian Standard Bible).

After doing a word study on the meaning of *sheep*, we learned that one simple meaning was *something that walks forward*. I emphasized to my children just how hard it is to be a shepherd versus being a sheep. A sheep has only one job, to hear instructions and move forward, make progress. By contrast, a shepherd must not only diligently and lovingly watch over the sheep in his care but also keep himself walking in the character of Jesus Christ.

I made up a new chart. For every task, there was a shepherd and one or two sheep. Each child had one job where he or she was the shepherd, the one who got to tell everybody else what to do. The honor of that title carried with it the responsibility that he or she was to practice the

Biblical standard for being a good shepherd. For the next task, the former shepherd knew he or she was to practice being a good sheep under a duly appointed sibling shepherd. He or she was to hear the shepherd's voice and obey.

All plans conceived in the mind of Christ work. The strife over jobs was reduced so dramatically that to this day I consider it one of the most successful scriptural lessons I ever taught. When you have 11 children, a victory like this feels like a gold medal at the Olympic games.

Our family's trajectory was on an upward climb. We were healthy, had jobs, loved and worked, played and prayed together. Through straitened financial circumstances and arduous work situations, we had carved out a life in New York and were the stronger for it. The external forces of growth, transition and relocation had bound us together. Soon coming internal pressures would tear us apart.

Chapter 9 | **A Companion for Control**

When Howard reached his mid-60's, he slowed his work schedule and moved into semi-retirement. This should have been a blessed time for all of us. Howard would have the opportunity to spend more time with his younger children, teaching them his skills in a fun, relaxed setting. With the children growing old enough to be more independent, Howard and I would have time to renew our sense of us.

That didn't happen. Instead, Howard, choice by choice, began to revert to a single life mentality. It is astonishing, even shocking, how quickly the heart hardens, even towards those closest to you, when self is elevated to the position of number one.

Selfishness and stinginess that had been relatively dormant in Howard now began to grow and strangle our relationship. A few years previously Howard had launched a vending business to increase the family income. He and I traveled together once a week to service the machines. Howard's transformation from husband and father into

Scrooge manifested one summer afternoon as we drove home from a vending route. I was in the back seat of the car counting and packaging coins. I asked Howard for a small amount of money to pay for a homeschool event for our children. My request was quite nominal compared to the funds Howard had spent wholly on himself in recent weeks. I did not foresee an issue.

Howard parked at a gas station to buy a cup of coffee. He turned, held a dime between thumb and forefinger, looked me in the eyes and announced, "I'm not going to give you one thin dime."

As Howard stepped out of the car on one side, I stepped out the other side and told him to go on without me, that I would walk the remaining five miles home. He drove off and I began my trek. Stopping off in the woods by the side of the road I spent an hour sitting on the trunk of a fallen tree, waiting on God.

The Lord said to me, "Howard is telling you the truth, Karen. He's not going to **give** you anything. When you or the children need money, you'll have to take it."

Throughout our nearly 30 years of marriage, I had tried to cultivate godly submission to Howard's authority, especially in regard to finances. I felt too weak to take a stand against Howard's covetousness and alter this entrenched pattern of relating. Compassionate to my frailty the Spirit gave me just a small step to take in this new direction. The step was so small I thought perhaps even Howard would agree it was reasonable. Mentally and spiritually fortifying myself I walked home.

Howard was in his man-cave completing the coin count. "I'm taking $15 per week out of the vending business as my allowance. I will spend it as the Lord leads me," I declared.

"No. Ridiculous. Unnecessary," Howard argued. I

stood fast, emboldened by the word I had received from the Lord.

This financial arrangement continued for years. In wonderful ways, God stretched that small amount of money like He multiplied the loaves and fishes in Bible times. It covered many of the children's activities, such as gymnastic lessons for our girls, homeschool trips, or new shoes. When I would request more funds for something extra or if Howard felt strained financially he essentially accused me of embezzling funds.

"Well, if you weren't taking $15 a week out of the household fund, maybe we'd have money for..."

I noticed a pattern on our vending days. Howard criticized everything I did -- the way I handled the soda cans, even the way I held the pencil to record the amount of product sold. Negative words have an effect, especially when spoken by someone in a position of authority over you. They become prophetic. Soon I was dropping cans and the pencil, manifesting oaf-like stupidity while Howard quietly, "tsk-tsked" me until I exploded. Then he would leave me alone.

Recognizing that Howard did this deliberately to feed his own idolatry of self I vowed every vending day, *I am NOT going to let him get to me today. I WILL NOT get angry and shout.*

Then I realized Howard wasn't satisfied until he had provoked me to anger. The only way to escape his withering criticism was to go ahead and yell at him, even if I wasn't angry. So, I yelled. It was shortly after that revelation that Howard turned the vending business over to me and I took one of the children with me every week.

It's been said that there are no secrets in the spirit. All motives are known at an unconscious level. Perhaps since Howard's intent had been uncovered there was no psychological benefit for him to oversee the business any longer.

Covetousness continued to fill Howard's heart. His mindset changed from being the family provider to resenting the drain his children and I made on his bank account. With his eye now turned inward, he began to look to his children to provide for him rather than the other way around. Our teenagers that still lived at home and had jobs paid their own auto insurance, auto maintenance bills, and cell phone bills, as well they should. But that financial independence by Joy, Lois and Jonathan was insufficient to satisfy the growing monster in Howard. To the monthly bill, he began adding "household contribution" for room and board.

Howard's modeling in money matters was thoroughly ingrained in his children. When James went on a cross-country bike trip, he stayed several weeks with relatives. He insisted, over their objections, on paying them room and board as he worked to earn money to continue his trip.

One of the most important duties of parents is to teach their children fiscal wisdom. The sooner children learn how to handle money, the better their chance of thriving in the real world. It wasn't the fact of our children paying their own way that was unjust. It was Howard's attitude about it. Our teens came to dread the summons as Howard presented them with their monthly bill.

There is no reasoning with unabashed, naked covetousness. Howard would gladly have taken every dime our children made, put it into the household account informing them, "When you need something, ask for it." That really meant, "Beg for it."

Requestng money from Howard meant enduring interrogation. "How much do you need? What do you need it for? I'm sure you can do it cheaper." We all made our finances stretch as far as possible to avoid the pain of asking Howard for money.

Every year my sweet parents sent me a check for my birthday. The money had always been deposited in Howard's and my joint bank account without being earmarked for anything special. That April I handed my check over to Howard as I had done every other year. The following day the Lord spoke to me, "Take the check back. That money is yours to use."

As if to punctuate that those funds were solely mine, it was the first year my father wrote the check including my maiden name, Karen Kinzer Rode.

God was leading me to stand against Howard's greed. When I asked Howard to return my gift he responded, "I'm not returning your check and if you ask again, I'll tear it into tiny pieces, and you'll have to tape them back together if you want to cash it."

I walked away in stunned disbelief at this plunge into the ridiculous. A few days later sanity prevailed, and Howard returned my check. I used the funds to pay for art lessons for Joy and a field trip with our home school group to the Glenn H. Curtiss Aviation Museum in Hammondsport, NY.

Before we were married Howard had a wedding photography business which he had laid aside to pursue handyman entrepreneurship. In semi-retirement, Howard's love of photography was renewed, and he traveled to local parks to take pictures. Nothing wrong with that, except that he did it alone. I was too busy to go along, and I had no desire to. I resented that photography took Howard away from us.

This was the era when photography was moving from the use of film to digital. Howard came home excitedly one day exclaiming, "I met a man who wants to sell his entire darkroom set-up for only $900!"

Oh, God, no!

Our family unit was so fractured by that time, but I kept trying to glue us together. I suggested, "For that amount of money we could take a quality vacation and reunite us as a family."

We still had five of our eleven sons and daughters at home. Howard told me I was being selfish, purchased the equipment and spent more hours away from us setting up his darkroom. In the end, he never used it. The regrettable part was he had spent all that money on something so obsolete.

I was homeschooling, running the vending business, shopping, and cooking, organizing everything for the family and keeping the books. Howard increasingly had time on his hands to pursue money-making schemes advertised in magazines or on TV, stay up late, sleep in late and take photography trips. I was running ragged and Howard was oblivious.

One would think that with a newly rekindled passion for photography, Howard would enjoy taking photos of our family. Sadly, I can't recall any pictures he took of his children during those years. Howard withdrew more and more into self and the children and I were outside of his life. In his mind, our job was to make his new life more enjoyable. If we weren't contributing to his comfort, or if we required anything of him, Howard accused us of rebelling against his authority.

Another family had moved into the main church building. They had girls the same ages as our four and a group of them walked up the road to pick black raspberries. I was in the yard when I heard screams. Our neighbor girls ran to me sobbing and babbling incoherently, "Rachelle...car..."

Finally, I could get out of them that Rachelle had been hit by a car. Racing down the driveway and up the road I found nine-year-old Rachelle sitting in a neighbor's yard, the lady of the house attending her. The woman had called 911 and an ambulance was on the way.

Details of what had happened came gradually. The road dipped and curved through that wooded area. The girls were scattered, some on one side of the road, some on the other. Rachelle darted across the road to join her sisters just as a car rounded the bend. The car struck her a glancing blow, throwing her up onto the hood and then to the ground.

These were the days before cell phones. Not all family members could be immediately notified, but I was able to contact Miriam. Her boyfriend offered his motorcycle. They sped the 40 miles from Rochester to Conesus. Discovering that Rachelle had been transported to Strong's hospital, they broke the speed limit returning to Rochester. Our friends at the Mission prayed, Miriam and her boyfriend sat anxiously in the waiting room, I was in an emergency cubicle comforting Rachelle.

Everyone was on high alert. Everyone but Howard. I had no idea where he was. He had ceased communicating his whereabouts. Finally, I was able to reach him at home and apprise him of the accident. We had just received the doctor's assessment that Rachelle's injury was minor -- a broken collarbone. Upon hearing the news, Howard got in his car and drove in the opposite direction, to Letchworth Park to take photos. I was shocked. The disconnect was so pronounced and telling, even for Howard. It was the beginning of many similar slights.

Sam, Nate, and James had been lawn care specialists for the three acres of landscaping at the Mission. With their growing income working in construction, our young men purchased land and built their own home a few miles away from us. Miriam, Paul, and Sharon were working and attending college. The task of lawn maintenance fell to Joy, Lois, and Jonathan.

Howard ignored me and our children most of the time. We felt the sting of that rejection, but it was preferable to his attention which had become tyrannical. Extremes of domination and control that had been occasional before now became the norm. It evidenced in his training of Joy, Lois, and Jonathan in lawn care.

Howard had never been one to yell at his children, but his increasing self-centeredness brought out the worst in him. A mother whose family lived in the main building reported hearing Howard scream at his kids while repairing and fine-tuning the weed eaters. When I questioned him later, he explained that he did it deliberately so the residents at the Mission would hear him and know how rebellious and inept his children were. All it proved was how out of control he was. That mother confided in me that she became afraid of Howard after that incident and hid when she saw him at Sam's Club.

Howard drew a map of the property delineating what needed to be mowed and weed-eated first, second, etc. Every blade of grass over three acres of uneven terrain, some of it steep hills, was to be groomed with the care appropriate for a golf course.

The summer of 1999 I planned a family vacation. The older children took time off work. We were packed and just awaiting Joy, Lois and Jonathan's completion of the lawn job. Out of the 12-hour requirement to complete the mowing and weed-eating each week, they missed ½ hour of the work. Howard declared, "I'm canceling the vacation. You didn't get your work done."

That was one of a few times when the Holy Spirit enabled me to stand against Howard's domination in His strength, not in my fear and anger. I quietly informed Howard, "We're going on vacation with or without you."

Sam, Nate, and Miriam all had cars of their own. We had enough vehicles to transport everyone. Howard backed down. In tears, Joy, Lois, and Jonathan completed the work and we all left together.

I was torn. I wanted our children to learn obedience to authority, even unjust authority. I believed that to be the proper scriptural model. Furthermore, it's not wise for father and mother to be divided with regards to their children. But at what point should my duty to protect our children's mental and emotional well-being take precedence over Howard's authority?

Daily I teetered on the horns of this dilemma. When I intervened, I felt guilty for siding with a son or daughter against my husband. When I didn't intervene, I felt guilty for being complicit with blatant injustice. Many times, I was not in close enough proximity to do anything at all.

Joy, Lois, and Jonathan, teenagers at the time, developed their own way of coping -- laughter. One evening I went upstairs to find them all together with Jonathan performing his version of the late-night show. He imitated Howard, right down to his walk and mannerisms. Jonathan's sisters roared with laughter. I didn't want to promote disrespect of authority, but I had to laugh, too. Jonathan was genuinely funny. I thought to reprimand them and take a stand for appropriate deference to God-ordained authority, but I couldn't. Laughter was their pop-off valve of release in the pressure cooker of their lives. I could not deprive them of that.

Howard lived in the house but for all practical purposes I was a widow and our children were fatherless.

We watched a World Vision documentary on TV -- a fundraiser to support their ministry of care for needy orphans around the world. Howard wept in compassion for those foreign children. I sat across the room bewildered at how he could turn a blind eye to the orphans sitting in the same room with him. Granted, their physical needs were met, but it was as if he was incapable of seeing past food and water. They needed their father.

Ever increasing selfishness choked out any remaining joy Howard had found in being a dad. He began to express a victim mentality, not only at home but publicly as well. To clerks in local stores, he would confide, "I have eleven children," intoned with a sigh indicating that they were an overwhelming financial burden to him.

This was at a time when six of our children were out of the house, making their own way in life and requiring nothing from him. His half-truths spread around the community upset me no end. The gulf between Howard and the rest of the family was so pronounced even acquaintances began to notice. I got a report that he was frequently eating dinner alone at a local restaurant.

A mutual friend, who had noticed him there more than once asked, "Howard, where is Karen?" Howard shrugged, "Home, I guess."

Still, I tried to reach Howard. Hope sprang anew in my heart when in the winter of 2000 Sam gave us the gift card he received from the local lumber yard in gratitude for his patronage. The gift was a four-night vacation package with the option of several cities, one being Honolulu, Hawaii. What could be better to heal a marriage than a vacation in Hawaii? The potential of a second honeymoon created cautious optimism in me.

We bought the plane tickets and extended our trip to

seven days, spending the last three days in Maui. Howard eagerly planned for weeks for this trip to a photographer's paradise. One suitcase held photography equipment, including two tripods, just in case, and the other suitcase held our clothes.

On the plane, he paid for a movie to watch for himself. "You don't want to watch anything, do you?" he queried.

With past history fully embedded in my mind and wanting Howard to have the trip of a lifetime, I replied, "No, I'm fine." I believed he didn't want to spend even a few dollars on me, though a movie would have been a welcome time filler on the nine-hour flight.

For six days I was Howard's photography assistant, which meant I was his pack animal carrying all his equipment as he raced around taking pictures. I brooded silently and refrained from complaining. Our final night in Maui Howard had not yet accomplished his ultimate picture-taking goal—a perfect sunset view over the ocean. I had waited and waited, hoping every day that his hunger for photos would be satiated and he would finally pay attention to me. We had one night remaining. I wanted one night, just one night, to sit on the beach with my husband watching the sun go down together. No pictures, no distractions, just us.

That scenario meant a great deal to me. But my mild request, "I'd like to sit on the beach together tonight..." did not dissuade Howard from his mission.

Had I communicated my desire more fully, would it have made a difference? Perhaps.

Howard went off in one direction on the beach, I went in the other. By the time we rendezvoused, I was spitting angry.

Just one night! That's all I desired... after giving him

everything he's wanted for six days he can't give me two hours!

  I walked angrily away, and Howard fell in behind me. Glancing back, I saw Howard parodying my clumsiness in the sand, mocking me in front of everyone on the beach.

  We managed to eat a final meal at a lovely restaurant that evening. The following morning, we ambled through a store waiting to be transported to the airport. The store displayed a tank where patrons could fish for pearls. We caught a pearl oyster, purchased the pearl and had it set in a dolphin charm which I wore on a necklace. Dolphins are symbols of unity. I clung to that necklace, hoping it symbolized a miracle ahead to save our marriage.

  Weeks turned to months, and months into years. Desperate to navigate this storm with the Lord I prayed, *God, help me love Howard.*

  When that prayer seemingly bore no fruit, my daily petition changed to, *God, I'm not going to try to love Howard anymore. That's not working. You are inside me and I know you are capable of loving even him. Please love him through me.*

  Neither did that prayer bring change or relief.

  Control had found companionship with greed in Howard's soul. Self-ruled as supreme potentate, turning Howard's once fruitful life into a moonscape, desolate and barren, without family and without love.

  Moon dust is as fine as flour and as rough as sandpaper. It penetrates the smallest crevices, pierces Kevlar-like material and gums up machinery. That's an apt description for what blew into our lives from Howard. I thought I was tough enough to survive the increasing stress, but I grieved for our children. The six of us steered clear of Howard as much as possible. In the summer of 2003, we were forced to abandon our strategy of avoidance when Howard's verbal abuse became physical.

Chapter 10 | **Lines Crossed**

Through the years that I had known Howard, he had shown himself a model of self-restraint and cool-headed practicality. I relied on him in a crisis. My family arrived for a visit in June 1993. Excited, eight-year-old Jonathan wanted to show his cousins the best time ever, so he took them on a tour of the nooks and crannies he had discovered in the Mission. I was in the yard when he came screaming out of the building running up the hill to our house. Sam intercepted Jonathan, took one look and exclaimed, "Oh, my God!"

    I have always felt inadequate to deal with physical trauma. Sam's outburst convinced me whatever had happened was horrific. Rather than run towards Jonathan, I ran the opposite direction to get Howard who was changing the oil in his work van. Jonathan had lifted a heavy metal grate to show his guests a hidden cavern in the bowels of the old building. The grate fell on his middle finger almost completely severing it. Only a scrap of skin held the end of his finger, from the knuckle out, to his hand. His fourth finger was smashed and flattened but whole.

We rushed Jonathan to the hospital. Howard stayed in the room as the surgeon reattached the finger. Blood and pain did not make Howard quail as it does me. Jonathan's screams reached the lobby and I could hardly bear it. I was grateful for Howard, grateful for his steady-as-you-go calmness in this harrowing situation. Through the doctor's skill and the body's ability to heal, surgery was successful. Today Jonathan has a functioning middle finger. The nail is somewhat disfigured and there is some loss of feeling in both his middle and fourth fingers, but they work.

In Howard's and my verbal battles, I was the one shouting, which made me look like the guiltier party. And sometimes I was the guiltier party, patrolling the waters of the enemy's territory, a battleship spoiling for a fight. At other times, Howard deliberately provoked me until I erupted so he could intone condescendingly, "K-a-r-e-n, wow, control yourself."

Only one argument early in our marriage became physical. Howard innocently asked me to locate a particular pair of scissors he had purchased. Fear exploded in my brain.

I have no idea where those scissors are. I haven't seen them in years, but Howard will never accept that answer. He'll keep drilling, insisting that I search until they are found.

I mounted a swift counter-attack to try to save myself from imagined relentless interrogation. The battle escalated until Howard threw me on the bed and put his forearm across my throat cutting off my air. My outrage turned to alarm.

I could die.

I gasped, "I can't breathe." Howard released me and left the room.

Now, years later, the conflict between us again broke out into bodily aggression. Sharon, home from college on school break, asserted her growing independence by mouthing off at her dad, resisting his absolute rule. And Howard gave her no quarter.

That was not always true. As a toddler, Sharon lolled blissfully on her daddy's lap luxuriating in his affection and munching on sunflower seeds she foraged from the cache in his shirt pocket. But now the former darling of Howard's heart became his nemesis.

More than once Howard suggested that I render heavy-handed justice to squash Sharon's rebellion. Not wanting to participate in what I believed was a disproportionate censure of our daughter I evaded the conversation. One morning I could no longer sidestep the issue. My husband demanded my cooperation, demanded that I align with him and discipline Sharon. I quietly voiced an alternate point of view.

Howard left the room where I was seated at my desk. Moments later a blow between my shoulder blades pitched me forward sending shock waves through my system. It felt like Howard slammed me with the heel of his hand.

"That's what you get for standing against me."

He wheeled and returned to the kitchen. The physical pain was negligible compared to the psychological pain. I felt the effects in my body for a few hours, but my inner self collapsed under this assault like a house in Tornado Alley taking a direct hit. Rebuilding my soul took days.

To be physically assaulted in the heat of an

explosive argument is one thing. To be ambushed and struck from behind for merely expressing a different opinion is quite another. I have read that verbal abuse unchecked often crosses the line to physical abuse. We had crossed that line. Gathering my scattered thoughts and emotions I reassembled them taking into account a new reality.

Howard's headship in our home had metastasized into a dictatorship. Our Bill of Rights was under attack. Over the next weeks freedom of speech, freedom to bear (verbal) arms to defend oneself, freedom to petition the government for a redress of grievances was pitted against our own King George III. Our George, like his predecessor, was willing to use violence to achieve lockstep compliance in thought, word, and deed. There were two contrasting lifestyles present and vying for supremacy. Two ideologies conflicted. One had to give way.

The temptation of Satan to Jesus was, "I'll give you everything you want if you fall down and worship ME" (Mt. 4:9). Jesus rejected the validity of that premise. My husband increasingly did not. He thought his life would be full, complete, peaceful, and prosperous if he got everything he wanted, if he put ME (himself) first.

It has been said that another way to spell Satan is S-e-l-f. Having experienced it, I agree. Elevating self to the position of a god means everyone in your realm of influence, in the vicinity of your idol, must conform to your whims or be sacrificed at the altar of your idol of ME. This lie of Satan, "Exalt yourself above the laws of God and you'll be god and have everything you want," is as old as the Garden and as new as the choices we all face every day.

When Jonathan was three-years-old many times a

day he would throw his arms around whatever part of Howard's body he could reach, hug him and gush, "Daddy, I love you."

His young son's magnanimity meant a great deal to Howard at that time, but Jonathan was a teenager. He still possessed what I believed was a divine gift of love for his dad, but Howard's self-absorption had so hardened his heart even the love of his youngest son couldn't penetrate it. In those trying years, I often admired Jonathan's patience and restraint with regards to his dad.

But even Jonathan had his limits. After work, Jonathan's escape was the computer. One evening I heard Howard go upstairs. Then pounding down the stairs -- Jonathan leaping them two at a time -- his trademark passage. Commotion in the living room. More movement up and down the stairs. Then shouting, scuffling, a physical fight. I sat frozen in my bedroom. Should I try to intervene? How could a weak woman get in between two angry men? A loud crash. Jonathan yelping. The back door opening and closing.

Later I found out the details. Howard went upstairs to insist Jonathan turn off the computer and go to bed. Jonathan refused so Howard began pulling out all the cables and packing them away. Enacting "an eye for an eye and a tooth for a tooth" retribution, Jonathan tore downstairs to disconnect Howard's VCR, cassette players and recorders housed in the living room console then returned to his bedroom.

Howard sauntered down the stairs and into the living room. Cables stuck out of his console and littered the floor like writhing snakes. Enraged, he stormed up the stairs, pulled Jonathan off his bed commanding him to reconnect the equipment. Jonathan fought back. The two wrestled to the top of the stairs and down to the corner landing.

Realizing his dad's superior strength and fearful of injury if Howard succeeded in hurling him down the stairs, Jonathan made the split-second decision to leap the ten steps to the first floor. He landed in a heap one foot twisted under him. Crying out he struggled to his feet and stumbled out into the night. Anxious moments followed. We didn't know where Jonathan was.

  Pain eventually forced him home. The three of us drove in icy silence to the emergency room. X-rays revealed a broken little toe. The bone healed improperly; the knuckle stuck up rubbing painfully on every shoe Jonathan wore. Years later it required corrective surgery. Though I know Howard did not deliberately set out to injure his son, neither did he express remorse. We were not surprised.

  After the incident with Jonathan, I feared for the physical safety of our children. Two years previously I completed Montessori teacher training and the remaining requirement for certification was a year's internship. A school in East Rochester hired me as an assistant teacher in a three to six-year-old classroom. This was mid-July. In a few weeks, my job would begin. From 7:00 a.m. until 5:00 p.m. five days a week I would be 35 miles away, our children left alone with Howard. Would I come home from work to find an injured child? The thought plagued my mind; worry troubled my heart. God sovereignly staged an intervention.

  Now in their late teens and early twenties, Joy, Lois, and Jonathan had full-time jobs with varying schedules and were seldom home at the same time. One morning, however, all were at the house. Susanna and Rachelle were 15 and 13-years-old. At my request, everyone congregated in the living room. One by one, through tears, our children poured out their hearts expressing their anguish at living in the same house with their father yet feeling fatherless.

Jonathan confessed, "I used to want a dad, but I don't think about it much anymore."

Howard was silent throughout the hour, then stood to leave. At the doorway, he paused, turned back and gave his answer to the cries of his children: "If you want my approval, do my will," and walked away. We were dazed. Howard's cold heart had grown even colder.

Matthew 19:6 says, "What therefore God has joined together, let no man separate" (NAS). But Howard was separating. He no longer desired the relationship of family. He resented the responsibility and complained about it publicly. The negative witness to the community at large and as a representative of our Christian fellowship could not continue to be ignored.

A few weeks after the family intervention the Holy Spirit made another attempt to convict Howard and bring him to repentance. In a prayer meeting at our church, Howard was exhorted to apply to himself the warning God gives to Israel in Jeremiah.

> How can you say, We are wise, and we have the written law of the Lord [and are learned in its language and teachings] . . .
>
> The wise men shall be put to shame; they shall be dismayed and taken [captive]. Behold, they have rejected the word of the Lord, And what wisdom and broad, full intelligence is in them?
>
> Therefore, will I give their wives to others and their fields to those who gain possession of them; for everyone, from the least to the greatest, is given to covetousness... (Jer. 8:8-10, AMP).

Very pointedly Lydia said, "Howard, God declares

in His Word that He takes the wives away from the covetous."

"Yeah, that's not going to happen." Howard had an unshakable confidence that his fiefdom would last forever. How very wrong he was.

Days later Lois moved 24 miles away to Pittsford to work as a live-in stable hand for five horses. I hired someone to refinish the hardwood floors in our house. The job required the application of several coats of varnish. Not wanting to inhale the fumes, I arranged for Joy, Jonathan, Susanna, Rachelle and I to stay at the Mission for a few days. Howard opted to remain at home. Bags packed the five of us headed out the door. I had no clue we would never return.

Chapter 11 | **Goodbyes**

The leadership of our Christian fellowship recognized Howard's and my mini-separation as portending something larger. They suggested I remain at the Mission and seek God regarding my future. My teaching job was to begin shortly. Living at the Mission meant my children would be protected from potential physical abuse by their father. We all chose to stay. I was unutterably thankful knowing that my children would be safe while I worked.

The Lord is always and forever merciful. The leadership of the church allowed Howard to remain living in the house on the hill. We all hoped and prayed for a quality change of heart, evidence of true repentance in Howard. After three months and no modification, not even the slightest indication of a desire to change, Howard was asked to leave the church property. He moved to a house in nearby Geneseo. God gave him what he had coveted for years — a single life. Howard was free of all responsibility, with all his time and money to use completely and wholly on himself, except for a minimal amount of child support he sent for Susanna and Rachelle.

Mercy from God encompassed us all. Mercy on Howard to end his abuse of power and prevent him from harming his children any further. Mercy on me to live life anew. Mercy on our children to fill the gap Howard left in their lives by being an absentee father.

The six of us -- Joy, Lois, Jonathan, Susanna, Rachelle and I -- attended a conference at the Mission. A man and his wife who had two young sons of their own had been seeking God about adopting a child.

This father had never met Jonathan but was so moved with compassion on his fatherless state that he declared, "You don't know me, Jonathan, but I love you."

This family took my 18-year-old son on vacation with them and then invited him to live with them. Jonathan stayed with them for seven months experiencing what he had not had at home — a godly father who genuinely loved him.

This same man in this same conference meeting stood in proxy for Howard and as a father repented to Lois. She flew into his arms and sobbed. Joy changed jobs and began working at the same company as a man whose family also lived at the Mission. This father had the opposite personality as Howard. He was kind, loving, fun, and forgiving. Sometimes Joy rode to work with him. God used the Body to heal us, its wounded members.

Shortly after Howard's and my separation, I lay on my bed in tears. *It's not supposed to end this way.*

No, it's not, but sometimes it does. And God brought this scripture to mind, "Many times I wanted to gather your people as a hen gathers her chicks under her wings, but you would not let me." (Lk. 13:34, New Century Version)

The Spirit spoke to my heart, "I knew how hard it would be for you to live with Howard. I made provision under My wings for you, but at times you just wouldn't come."

True. I believed God thought about me the same way Howard did. I didn't measure up to Howard's standard of perfection in the natural. Projecting that image onto God I believed He also held up an unattainable spiritual standard that I failed to meet. I was double-minded. On the one hand, I trusted God, prayed continuously, heard His voice on occasion and obeyed to the best of my ability. On the other hand, remnants of generational distrust of men remained and I felt I had evidence to prove that God favored men over women. That conviction blocked the succor Jesus would gladly have provided during those especially difficult years with Howard.

This new season of life was both happy and heartbreaking. Our older children, Sam, Nate, Miriam, James, Sharon and Paul had moved on with their lives, starting businesses, going to Bible school, enrolling in college. With the busyness of their lives, they were largely unaware or in denial of the increasing turbulence on the home front in the years leading up to Howard's and my separation.

Their belief was, "We all took it from Dad in our teenage years. It's just a rite of passage. Nothing to worry about."

With me living at the Mission, teaching full-time and absorbed in the work of the ministry, and Howard and I estranged, the gulf widened between me and our older children. We had little contact with them. Jonathan and Lois were living off site, but we saw them at the Saturday night youth prayer meetings. Joy, Susanna, Rachelle and I were swaddled in safety physically and emotionally at the

Mission. We were healing but our family was fractured. Grief and loss mingled with our peace.

Joy found work as a cook's helper at the Big Tree Inn in Geneseo which piqued her interest in cooking. She learned to make festive salads and fancy desserts. Training as a sauté chef, she discovered that Alfredo sauce is not some exotic concoction that only appears in expensive restaurants. It can be whipped up fresh in a home kitchen with just a few ingredients.

With me working full-time, Susanna took on the role of family chef. She and Joy worked out a schedule -- Susanna planned and cooked weekdays, Joy weekends. In her new role, Susanna experimented with a variety of recipes. The arguments in the kitchen about how some dish should be prepared, Joy's restaurant way, or Susanna's cookbook way, turned into a stiff competition of "Who's the best chef?"

I was the beneficiary. Delicious dinners awaited me when I arrived home from work each night and my daughters packed my lunch with leftovers for the next day. The aroma of my five-star restaurant worthy meals wafting through the teacher's lunchroom made my colleagues drool with envy.

Daughters are psychologically wired to grow into strong, confident women basking in the sunshine of their father's approval. But Howard admired male strength. He often stated, especially in the years leading up to our separation, "I've observed that women possess about half the strength of men."

I felt his declaration really meant women are half -- in every respect. Every daughter longs for her dad's approbation. Knowing femininity held little value in Howard's kingdom, this attitude had squelched Joy's and Lois' emerging womanliness. With the encouragement and prayers of mothers and grandmothers at the Mission, the desert of femininity in my girls began to blossom like a rose. They became vibrant, beautiful women.

My own sense of femininity also flourished and found an outlet in redecorating my bedroom. Though I had the liberty to beautify our homes through the years, I had always felt very inadequate in that womanly art. My excuse was that I was busy raising the children and had little time or money to pursue such niceties. Joy enrolled in a correspondence course in interior decorating and needed an actual room to renovate to complete an assignment. I gave her my credit card with no restrictions and told her I wanted my bedroom to look like a garden to allay the long New York winters and give me a sense of peace and beauty when I came home from work.

Joy painted the walls a pale mint green and installed a forest green carpet. I splurged on a new dresser, nightstand, and a distinctive secretary with an intricate pattern of inlaid wood. Two bookcases and a corner shelving unit completed the furniture requirements. At JoAnn's, Joy and I selected a painting of a garden scene and had it framed. Establishing the secretary as the focal point in the room, Joy garnished the top with an arrangement of purple and white candles on a crystal platter and hung the painting just above her creation. That inspiring view filled my vision as I lay in bed. I love wisteria and I purchased garlands of it to wind around the two standing lamps in the room. Joy's labor of love and the garden haven she created in my bedroom made it very precious to me.

When Rachelle turned 15 God arranged for me to take a year off from teaching to concentrate on her delayed development. To make up for the loss in income the parents in the fellowship hired me to help them homeschool their children. It was a gracious and generous offer, a wonderful gift of charity to help me with Rachelle. I signed up with the Christian Association of Neurodevelopmentalists. The specialist tested Rachelle to ascertain how her brain processed information, then designed a program specific to her. It covered academics, physical exercise, attention, and focus. The exercises corrected her auditory processing issue and sensory deficiency. It was a rigorous program requiring all day to complete and Rachelle made astounding progress those first six months. I was tremendously encouraged.

Occasionally we heard from Howard. My daughters and I were still very bruised from his excessive domination. We feared contact and we did not meet with him even when he bribed Susanna with a promise of money if she would have dinner with him. Our trained responses to do his will resided strongly in us. If we met Howard face to face, we doubted we would have the strength to stand against his wishes.

Indeed, one of the intercessors in our fellowship once told Howard, "It's not enough that your family does your will. They already obey your will. Your domination finds its greatest satisfaction when you feel you have forced someone to do your will."

I believe that assessment is accurate. It explains dynamics that otherwise defy reason.

After two and a half years of living at the Mission God sovereignly moved again. In April 2006, during the night, a torrent of the Father's love and power washed over me. Wave after wave crashed around, in and through me. Over and over, on and on power flooded my being until it seemed more than I could bear, but I didn't want it to stop. It may have only lasted a minute, but that kind of power is like high voltage electricity going through a person.

Moments seem like hours. I had no understanding of why God so visited me.

Meanwhile, I had hit a plateau with Rachelle. Her neurological program required six hours of work five days a week. Sometimes Rachelle fought me to a standstill, and I had to discontinue the schedule for a few days. When we returned to the lessons, her effort was lackluster. Her heart was not in the work. Assessments confirmed Rachelle was no longer making progress. Her emotional responses remained immature and she was even slipping backward into increasing childishness. I was desperate to stop her backward slide. Rachelle's drive to control me was keeping her stuck in immaturity. She felt secure in her place as a dependent child forcing me to be her caregiver.

Bringing the situation to the fellowship for corporate prayer Barbara suggested an alternative that surprised us all. For her own benefit, Rachelle needed to separate from me. Further prayer and consideration brought consensus that this directive was wisdom from God.

I researched boarding schools online. They were all elite prep schools, out of the question for my academically challenged daughter. There was one exception -- a Christian school for troubled teens in Indiana. It wasn't a perfect fit. Rachelle did not have the usual troubled teen profile of drugs and rebellion. However, another teen we knew had attended this school and had benefited from the experience.

After contacting the school, they interviewed Rachelle. Though her history did not fit their norm, they were willing to accommodate her. In June 2006, shortly before Rachelle's 16th birthday, I dropped her off at New Creations. It was a sudden uprooting of everything familiar to Rachelle.

I was grateful for the encouragement of one of the

students in residence. She told Rachelle, "At first you'll hate it here, but then you'll love it." That proved to be true.

This tearing asunder of the intense relationship I had with Rachelle also sent shock waves through my system. For the first time in 34 years, I had no constraint on my time and energies. I had no husband to serve and no dependent children. For two and a half years, I had basked in freedom from stress and worry, success in teaching, and joyous companionship with my daughters and my friends. Summer vacation from teaching and an empty nest thrust me into unfamiliar territory. I felt in limbo. For no reason that I could discern, contentment and happiness dissipated more and more with each passing day. I prayed endlessly trying to regain a sense of wholeness.

My increasing disquietude became obvious to the leadership at the Mission. They suggested perhaps it was time for me to consider a different path for my life.

A different path?! I have been associated with this group of people for 36 years.

As with the children of Israel, we had walked through the Red Sea, across the desert and seen the miracles of God together. This community was my security, my lifeline to God. I clung desperately to this life I had known, convinced that I could not survive without it.

God, I can't make this decision. You make it for me.

Expecting to teach at the Mission again in September, I spent those summer days developing a new curriculum combining Bible, science and history. In August my former boss at the Montessori school called. My colleague who I had worked with for three years was moving to Florida. Would I come back and teach, not as an assistant, but as a head teacher?

I didn't want to. I felt so privileged, so holy staying at the Mission overseeing the home school education there.

Howard had realized his dream life. So had I. I was living a holy life in a holy place doing holy work. In my imagination, I had finally achieved the honor of being a set-apart spiritual being, closer to God than ordinary people -- a nun with the added bonus of children.

Informing Lydia about the phone call and job offer, which I judged to be a lure from Satan to pull me out of God's will, she surprised me with, "Take the job."

To me, that meant I had failed to be spiritual enough, holy enough. I wasn't qualified to teach the Christian children at the Mission. Lydia softened the blow with the proposal that I could still teach at the Mission on weekends and holidays. She thought my job would be a temporary assignment off grounds, a pause to give me time to remedy my faulty spiritual condition.

Reluctantly, I accepted the job and identified with King Nebuchadnezzar in the Bible who was ousted from his palace because of his arrogance and rebellion against God. Nebuchadnezzar wandered as a beast in the forest for seven years. At the end of that time he declared, "...my understanding and the right use of my mind returned to me; and I blessed the Most High God" (Dan. 4:34 AMP). And God restored Nebuchadnezzar to the throne of Babylon.

Surely, I had more going for me than that ancient heathen king. Surely, I too, would be restored to my former exalted estate if I just tried hard enough. I forced myself to listen to Bible tapes on the 45-minute drive to and from work and spent all my leisure time in a prayer room.

But strain continued to develop between me and my friends which could neither be ignored nor breached. I tried every way I knew to bridge the gap. It was especially frustrating because there was no outward pressure to blame. I had no disagreements, no arguments with my fellow prayer partners. All of my efforts at both inner and outer reconciliation proved futile. The surface was placid, but beneath the calm a storm raged. The alienation in the spirit seemed to affect the atmosphere in the prayer meetings and I was asked not to attend. It was a death knell. Anyone else so censured had never been reinstated into our tightly knit group.

I had observed and participated in the separation of people from our Christian fellowship in previous years. It followed a distinct pattern. The leadership brought up this person's seeming inability to fully engage in the direction they believed God was directing the group. There was prayer and communication, both with the individual and among ourselves. We held out hope that there would be change, motion forward on the part of the person in question. When it seemed that did not happen after several weeks or months, that person was asked to leave.

Once the decision was made there was the immediate withdrawal of all friendship, comfort, and help. The individual was considered an Absalom -- someone in defiance of God-ordained authority who could entice and tempt others to rebel. This person -- a blight, a pariah, a force for evil -- could not be disposed of quickly enough. Even his possessions were considered tainted. Any gift the person had given to a member of the fellowship was thrown away. It was a tie to the one being sent away and potentially had negative spiritual power -- like the negative power that often affixes itself to idols purchased in foreign countries.

I did everything I could to stave off this impending doom. Reading my Bible, begging God to help me. When that bore no fruit, I attempted to run away. I told the elders I would move to Washington to care for my invalid mother.

God shut that door when my brother said, "We have

no funds to support you if you come."

All detours were blocked. There was only one way out, through the same gauntlet that others had run through.

The crisis came -- summoned to the prayer meeting -- told to leave. I had four days to move out. I called moving companies. None could come on Veteran's Day weekend and on such short notice. I pleaded. Finally, one agreed to come and carry my furniture to a self-storage unit.

A mind riddled with fear and lies does not make intelligent decisions. I believed my life and my possessions had been condemned by God. Hating myself I turned the vitriol into ruthless discarding of my belongings, even things that were precious to me. Into the dumpster went the sole copy of piano arrangements I had created for Edith's original songs. Into a bonfire went the garlands of wisteria I had draped around my bedroom.

I knew if I left any shred of me anywhere in the facility it would be announced in a meeting, "Karen left this on purpose so as to have a connection, a backdoor in, a way to continue to frustrate our efforts. This is the source of the spiritual warfare we've been experiencing in our meetings." It had been said about others who had left.

I finalized the massive purge by throwing away the six large notebooks I had created in my two years of Montessori training. They represented hundreds of hours of work. Then the Holy Spirit spoke. One clear instruction, a pinpoint of light shining into the black chaos of my mind, "Karen, don't throw your life away." I reached into the dumpster and retrieved those notebooks.

Susanna had just turned 18, Joy was 24. Their mother, whose history with this fellowship went back almost to its inception, who was considered by all to be part of the inner circle, was cast out. What were they to think? What were they to do with this further earthquake and rupture in the life of our family? They were not exiles. They were not rejected. There was no time for my daughters to process this shock. They would remain at the Mission in the only home they had ever known, now essentially orphans, severed in relationship from both mother and father.

In every previous case at the Mission, the assessment of "Why did this person leave?" concluded with, "They left because they failed to meet the requirements of radically following Christ."

In essence, such a person was branded with a scarlet "F" for failure. Their name was erased from conversation and from the history books of the Mission. My daughters would now have to endure watching their mother's name and reputation as a servant of God be besmirched as their father's had been three years earlier.

My car was packed. Joy and Susanna stood with me at the back door of the Mission — the three of us with emotions too raw and too stunned to react even with tears. It's possible to be physically beaten to the point nerves become numb and you can't feel the blows anymore. That's the way my emotions felt -- numbed by the blows of this circumstance.

A quick hug goodbye and I got in my car. To look at my daughters' faces in the rearview mirror as I drove away was torment. I had to turn against and deny my mother's heart which the Lord had worked so hard to develop in me.

God does not leave His beloved bereft. The baptism of love I had experienced six months previously had prepared me for this extreme situation. And my Helper had answered my prayer, "I can't make the decision to leave this group I have been associated with for most of my adult life. You make it for me."

A year or so later after leaving the Mission a prophet said to me, "God drop-kicked you out of the arena."

Yes, He surely did. But it was many months before I could receive the comfort of that baptism and God's taking over my life in such a dramatic way. In the meantime, I faced deep soul darkness, such as I had never known before.

Chapter 12 | **Love One Another**

Why had Howard and I become so involved in the deliverance church?

Ministry dynamics are sometimes difficult to process and hard to explain. Some might read my story and think, "This organization is a cult."

Others might look at the love and fellowship we experienced and think, "I wish I was part of a tight-knit community like that."

I've had time to reflect on my 36 years with this fellowship of believers. Those years were both wonderful and glorious, painful and messy.

On the glorious side of things, I believe people are drawn to deliverance ministries for two reasons: 1) Dysfunctions in their own lives are not healed in traditional church meetings and 2) they sincerely want to help others in such dilemmas.

Howard came to the ministry after breaking down in the army. Stationed in San Francisco during the Korean conflict, he played in the army band that sent the ships off to war and welcomed them home. Although Howard did not experience overseas deployment in wartime, his inner conflicts caused him to admit himself into a veteran's mental facility. After several months he was honorably discharged with a diagnosis of schizophrenia. Howard then attended Bible College and later worked as a draftsman for San Joaquin County. He studied or worked in these situations only 18 months. After that length of time, internal pressures built, and he quit school and his job.

Knowing Howard's problems, a fellow believer told him of a deliverance meeting in Modesto, California, 40 miles from his home in Lodi. The friend had disposed of the advertisement, but he knew the meeting would be held at a lodge at 2:00 pm on Sunday afternoon. In an uncharacteristic burst of faith, Howard decided to trust God to get him to that meeting.

He prayed, "Lord, You're in me. I'm going to drive to Modesto and believe You will get me to that meeting."

Howard felt a power come on his foot controlling his speed. He sped up, then slowed down all the way to Modesto. Arriving in the city his eye caught a car passing in front of him in the cross street.

He recognized the driver as a fellow Christian and concluded, "I bet they're going to the same meeting." Howard made a right-hand turn and followed them to Pastor Ben's meeting.

In personal ministry that day, God gave Ben a vision of Howard's brain. Instead of normal rhythmic brain wave patterns, Ben saw brain waves shooting chaotically all over the place. The understanding by the Spirit was this malfunction happened due to drugs Howard's mother took during labor. For some reason, the drugs went to Howard's brain affecting it negatively.

Through the laying on of hands and prayer this and other emotional distresses were discerned and miraculously corrected. The fact that Howard married, launched successful businesses in California and New York and supported a large family gives credence to the efficacy of deliverance ministry.

Prayer brought miraculous intervention to me in 1971. I was a green, first-year teacher of eighth-grade history and English in the Spokane Valley school district. During spring break, I traveled to California to attend Ben's meetings. I shared the difficulty I was having with one of my students. Coming from a dysfunctional home, Charlie garnered attention by being loud and disruptive in class.

When the class was settled and quiet, Charlie would shout from the back of the room, "What page are we supposed to be on?" All teachers had the same experience with Charlie. He was intelligent but earned D's and F's in every class.

I tried various approaches to solve my problem with Charlie. I put his desk in the back of the room, I ignored his outbursts, I even exiled him to the hall. Nothing worked.

My latest effort had been to put his desk right in front of mine reasoning, *Since I can't stop Charlie from talking, I'll put him right in front of me, so his conversation doesn't disturb the rest of the class.*

That didn't work either. Charlie was as loud as ever, constantly disrupting the class.

Over spring break, I attended meetings with Pastor Ben. I laughed as I told Ben my experience with Charlie. "I don't think you're as happy as you pretend to be," Ben responded. "You want to be successful and that boy is making you look bad. And he knows you're mad at him.

Makes him nervous. That's why he talks all the time."

It was true. I hated that Charlie made me look weak and ineffective. I prayed all night asking God to cleanse my heart of anger towards Charlie.

Returning to class a few days later I did not admonish Charlie to be quiet or attempt to alter his behavior in any way. Yet for those remaining six weeks of school, Charlie was a model student. Not once did he disrupt class. Furthermore, he earned A's and B's in all his work for me. The ultimate blessing came on the last day of school. Charlie was the only one of my students to stop by my room and gift me with his picture.

Clearing my own spirit from anger towards Charlie made possible a flow of the love of God to him and he responded. Basking in the sunshine of God's love nourished Charlie's soul and released his mind to function to its capability. And it was all accomplished as a change at the spirit level. I did nothing overtly to effect this transformation. This first-hand experience of deliverance prayer impressed me very much.

Earlier chapters recount my dysfunction with men that drew me to the deliverance ministry. Howard and I both believed that without the help we received from Pastor Ben and Lydia we could not have married and raised a family. Though our family life was not perfect, we felt the deliverance church gave us and our children a strong Biblical foundation on which to build successful lives.

Life at the Mission was, at its best, heaven come to earth. Our Christian fellowship made every attempt to live out the word of God. "This is my commandment, that you love one another as I have loved you," Jesus said (Jn. 15:12 English Standard Version) "Therefore, confess your sins to each other and pray for each other so that you may be healed. The prayer of a righteous person is powerful and effective," wrote James (Jms. 5:16 NIV).

Our meetings focused on healing — not only healing of the body, but also of the mind and spirit. Thorny, complicated situations and relationships require wisdom from God to discover His path of healing for each unique circumstance. It was not uncommon for us to pray an hour or more for just one person's need.

Prayer, for us, was a part-time job added to our ordinary lives. We gathered several nights a week for three or four hours of prayer. This in addition to our own private devotions. It was a life of prayer and fasting. We fasted from down time evening activities such as watching TV or playing games or socializing in order to pray.

Our prayer list included leaders in government and in the church as well as our own families. We prayed on phone conferences with people we had never met who heard help was a phone call away. Our leaders fearlessly tackled the most convoluted entanglements in people's lives. They believed God truly is Almighty and that He will lead every seeker to higher ground no matter the morass in which they are ensnared.

I marveled at the love, kindness, mercy, insight and counsel offered by our team to a woman who called in anonymously to receive help because she had had an affair with her husband's best friend.

Most healings of body and soul in our ministry happened gradually over time, but miraculous healings sometimes occurred. Paul Basile lived and worked in New York City. He and his brothers owned a construction business. Two men from the Mission had just arrived at a job site to begin working for Paul. As he turned from a boiling vat of tar he was tending and strode towards his friends to greet them the tar exploded, and Paul was engulfed in a ball of fire.

Flames extinguished, Paul asked to be taken to the on-site office where he called the Mission for prayer. Ben and Lydia were in residence at that time and convened an emergency meeting. The 25 mostly women and children gathered, and we poured out our hearts in prayer for this brother who we loved.

Fifteen minutes later we heard these unbelievable words from Paul, "Ben, the pain's all gone."

Rather than go to a hospital, Paul went home. He had suffered first, second and third degree burns over much of his body, especially the backs of his legs. Encouraged by stories of other burn victims who had recovered using home remedies, Paul bathed and scraped his burned flesh. We continued to pray for him when he experienced discomfort and he never again felt the searing pain of the initial accident. Six weeks later Paul returned to work, his skin healed without a single scar. A total and complete miracle.

At its best, our Christian fellowship loved. We loved each other enough to convene on a moment's notice to pray when one of us had a need. Family celebrations were interrupted on Christmas Eve the year one of our members had a financial need. When I began working full-time leaving Susanna and Rachelle at the Mission, another family invited my daughters to eat lunch with them every day. On school holidays I reciprocated by cooking for their family. The sharing of home-cooked meals and sweet fellowship forged bonds and memories dear to all of us.

The closeness of our fellowship wrapped us in the blessings of family. Since Howard's and my relatives lived in Washington, California, Wisconsin, and Minnesota, the church family became our children's grandparents, aunts and uncles, cousins and best friends. The love and value extended to our sons by other men in the fellowship offset the harshness they received from their father. Howard's disregard of his daughters' femininity the ladies balanced by encouraging them to express womanliness in dress, manners and deportment. And I had the support, prayers, and counsel of older women in the raising of our children.

Prayer meetings, communion services, campfires, picnics, celebrations, mission trips united us. One communion service instead of the traditional flat wafers we had a loaf of French bread. Each man, woman, and child tore off a piece and fed it to another. It didn't matter how many pieces of bread one received. No one was counting. We were too busy laughing, loving each other, seeing how many people we could feed. Love and the glory of God flowed like new wine -- effervescent and life-giving.

I especially appreciated the care given our older members as they made their transition from this life to the next. Those that didn't require hospitalization were loved, prayed for, attended to 24/7 by a rotating team of their spiritual family until they passed peacefully into the arms of Jesus.

In 1994, at the age of 80, Pastor Ben developed bone cancer. A few weeks before he died those from across the country who had benefited from his ministry gathered on a phone conference and one by one expressed their gratitude for his faithfulness and service. Memorial services are one of my favorite memories from my time in the deliverance ministry. We laughed and cried together reciting funny and heartwarming incidents in our comrades' lives, knowing they were in eternity, still united with us in love just on the other side of a thin veil.

The deliverance ministry has disbanded, and many members are now deceased. Those of us who remain are scattered across the United States and not often in touch. I heard Paul Keith Davis give an account of experiencing the outer courts of heaven while enduring back surgery.

When Paul inquired of the Lord about this seeming impossibility Jesus told him the love and prayers of his friends and family had created that atmosphere. The love of Christian brothers and sisters is, in reality, the outer courts of heaven.

We experienced those outer courts of heaven and retain a closeness that spans the miles and has endured through the years. I have read that the strongest bonds between people are forged from experiencing the glory of God together or suffering the extremes of war together. In the deliverance ministry, we experienced both glory and war.

Chapter 13 | **Prisoner of War**

Life at the Mission was, at its worst, nothing like heaven. It was more like war. To seek the kind of knowledge and power from God that delivers is a noble ambition. Accurate discernment is required coupled with uncommon love and a willingness to confront sin. Deliverance is rich with potential for good, but also fraught with possibility for harm because, in the end, people are flawed.

> The sinful nature wants to do evil, which is just the opposite of what the Spirit wants. And the Spirit gives us desires that are the opposite of what the sinful nature desires. **These two forces are constantly fighting each other,** so you are not free to carry out your good intentions" (Gal. 5:17 New Living Translation).

The battle between good and evil, whether fought within an individual or in society is an all-out, take no prisoners, fight to the death conflict.

We in the deliverance ministry voluntarily entered this war with the intent of helping each other fight the enemy within. But, as in a natural war, there were casualties. Leaders made mistakes. Soldiers were wounded by friendly fire.

People from out of state arrived at the Mission for a special weekend conference. Hope and inspiration rose high in the meeting Friday night. It seemed easy to "...strip off and throw aside every encumbrance and the sin which so readily clings to and entangles us, and... run…" (Heb. 12:1 AMP).

A ladies' prayer session was announced for Saturday afternoon. I was stoked. I was beyond ready. I couldn't wait. All morning I thought, *Just give me a chance on that prayer chair. I know I'll give up every hindrance that keeps me from being more like Jesus.*

The room was filled with perhaps twenty other women. I was so anxious I wished I was first. I chafed, waiting for my turn as one lady after another sat on the prayer chair in the middle of the room while everyone prayed for discernment of what barriers might be keeping that person from a more perfect union with Christ.

Finally, my time came. I eagerly sat down expecting accolades, roses strewn on my path, as I displayed my zealous pursuit of Christ. I would be shoulder to shoulder with the Apostle Paul, an example to the flock, able to proclaim with that saint. "You should imitate me, just as I imitate Christ" (1 Cor. 11:1 NKJV).

Instead, the combined discernment of the intercessors unveiled hidden rebellion in my spirit. Disbelief and horror mounted as on and on went the exposure that I was in direct defiance of God. Though I was not physically or consciously hurting anyone, so the charge went, the hidden motives of my heart held daggers to kill all imagined threats to my fancied superiority. Consequently, the Holy Spirit was taking the drastic measure of cutting off my spiritual arms and legs to keep me from doing any more harm.

Lydia declared, "Your hands will no longer be able to reach out to hurt anyone, but neither will you have the capacity to reach your hands out to help and nurture anyone. Your legs will no longer walk paths of self-worship and rebellion, but neither will you be able to walk with God during this season. Howard will carry you."

I was devastated, undone by this revelation. For months I lived under a pall of guilt and despondency. Only these years later do I have a more comprehensive and accurate understanding of that season. I presented my Pharisee persona to God for His approval and commendation. In response, He whetted His sword (Ezek. 21:15) to slaughter the image that was distorting the view of my true self. In God's eyes, that Pharisee image was as grotesque and aberrant as the images in a funny mirror house at a circus. I discovered, by experience, God's absolute and fierce hatred of lies, hypocrisy and sin that distorts His image, corrupting the person He created in the beginning.

"Behold, therefore, the goodness and severity of God…" (Rom. 11:22 KJV). The Greek word translated *severity* means *to cut abruptly, decisively.* I was not only beholding the decisive cutting of God - I was experiencing it.

Some may protest, "Oh, well, that's the nature of Father God. He's vindictive, but Jesus is sweet and kind and mild. He would NEVER do anything like that."

Jesus Himself said, "The Father and I are one." God the Father, God the Son and God the Holy Spirit are not divided. They are one spirit, one mind, one nature. "When you've seen me you've seen the Father," Jesus told Philip.

Jesus took the Pharisees to task at every turn, denouncing them as vipers, unmerciful, hypocrites, murderers, full of dead men's bones, strolling pompously around making followers more damned to hell than they themselves were (Mt. 23). Jesus executed severity on the Pharisees of His day, and He is the same yesterday, today and forever. If He did it then, He will do it again today. The severity of God nailed my Pharisee to a cross. As with crucifixion, it would be a slow and agonizing death.

It took time for me to believe in the goodness of God, to experience Jesus' overwhelming love and nurture of the real me, the lost me, the one He came to seek and to save (Lk. 19:10). Reflecting these years later I see God had utter and complete confidence in Himself, in His ability to keep me through the wilderness of despair that would follow this severity. Despair that though I knew my salvation was assured, felt that I would never be close to Jesus as I longed to be. I thought I would always and forever be far from the Father, on the outskirts of hell rather than the courts of heaven. It took time for Jesus to build up my inner person, the real me hidden in Him (Col. 3:3) and bring me eventually out into the wideness of His goodness and mercy.

The only thing real to me that Saturday afternoon at the prayer meeting was shock and humiliation. My own heart had betrayed me. How could there be such a chasm between my conscious thoughts and the ambitions of my spirit? That confrontation and other similar ones embarrassed me and filled me with doubt and dread. The elders, especially Lydia, had been very accurate in their discernment so many times in the past, how could I reject their words now? I couldn't.

The deliverance ministry, whose stated goal was to deliver seekers from the scourge of fear and doubt, instead began to fill me with those very torments. I began to distrust my own thoughts and fear my own heart. Judging by that prayer meeting and many similar ones, I had no knowledge of or control over my subconscious self that apparently was very evil.

I was living Jeremiah 17:9 (KJV), "The heart is deceitful above all things, and desperately wicked: who can know it?" Although I knew my trust was supposed to be in God, not people, I began to rely more and more on Lydia's and the elders' approval. Only in their affirmation did I feel acceptable to the Father.

This concept of a capricious God was the most challenging aspect of my experience in the deliverance ministry. God's love seemed as unreliable as the game we played as girls pulling petals off a daisy to determine the affections of a boy we fancied. Daily, hourly my mind pulled petals off of the daisy of God's acceptance, "He loves me, He loves me not," and most often the last petal was, "He loves me not."

Intellectually, we all agreed, "God loves sinners so much He sent Jesus to die for us. There is therefore now no condemnation" (Rom. 8:1). And "Whomever the Lord loves, he chastens so don't despise chastening" (Heb 12:6).

The words were said, but I did not feel loved, I felt condemned. I believed God had favorites and I wasn't one of them. It did seem He was fickle, ready to rebuke me for the slightest infraction and cast me off as a filthy garment. I believed if I didn't make good here amongst people who were sincerely seeking the highest and best of the Christian life, then there was no hope or redemption for me regardless of what the Bible said.

Our leaders painted the picture of our job as

intercessors. We were to be soldiers who slept in full battle gear with our fingers on the trigger of our weapons, ready to fight day or night. Gathering to pray at moment's notice was not unusual. To be led by the Spirit was our goal. Missing a meeting, for any reason, was regarded by our leaders as evidence we had not heard the Holy Spirit. Anxiety rose within me anytime I left the property, fearful I would miss a call for prayer at the Mission.

I was particularly happy one summer day as I drove my children to the theme park at Darien Lake. Scheduled outings that all families participated in were safe from censure even if we were absent from an emergency prayer meeting at the Mission. The prospect of freedom from fear for one entire day was joy indeed.

Arriving home, I received a call from Sharon asking me to stop by Taco Bell, pick up food and bring it to her boyfriend's work site. Desiring to revel in the ambiance of that sun-filled day as long as possible, I was glad to fill her request. I delivered the food, stayed and visited and laughed with Sharon and her friend for a short while. Arriving home later that night, I was met with the somber news that I had missed a prayer meeting, one that was of dire consequences to Miriam and myself.

At that time Miriam was living in Colorado Springs working in a new ministry job. Her credentials as a member of our church had opened the door for this opportunity and Miriam loved her work. New on the job, Miriam had made an innocent mistake, sharing information that had the potential to compromise our church's outreach in the area. Even though I knew nothing of the situation, I was accused of spiritually aiding and abetting her, with the hidden goal of destroying the ministry's work in Colorado Springs. We were likened to Herodias and Salome who conspired to behead John the

Baptist. The joy of the day evaporated, replaced by fear and dread. Miriam and I were judged guilty of treason and I, as the mother, bore the greater blame.

These were wounds from friendly fire. I had suffered many sword slashes and bullet wounds from friendly fire. But Miriam, who had always garnered praise for her competency in every job, was devastated. That prayer meeting began to unravel the cord that held Miriam to the fellowship. Several weeks later she was forced to make a decision to either stay in that job she loved or part ways with our fellowship. Under duress, Miriam chose to quit her job to stay with our church. Later, the elders dismissed her as spiritually unfit for the church's changing mission and severed their relationship with her. It took years for her to heal.

More than once this type of ambush threw me and others into despondency. Day to day, we never knew when one of us might be accused. We often entered prayer meetings with fear and trepidation, watching Lydia's face when she entered to gauge what kind of mood the Holy Spirit was in and who might be in trouble. Our goal became to stay out of trouble.

Why, one may ask, did you stay? Why did you accept those words of judgment?"

That's a hard question to answer to someone who wasn't there. I had watched others undergo such exposure. The ones who rejected the discernment, thinking themselves to be wise in their own minds, quite often became hardened, stuck in self-righteousness. Those who prayed through the discernment to a place of understanding and acceptance experienced new freedom in Christ.

I kept hanging on through the despair hoping to claim as mine the reality of Habakkuk 3: 19 (Amplified

Bible, Classic Edition): "The Lord God is my Strength, my personal bravery, and my invincible army; He makes my feet like hinds' feet and will make me to walk [not to stand still in terror, but to walk] and make [spiritual progress] upon my high places [of trouble, suffering, or responsibility]!"

Some injuries to my soul were self-inflicted. My *modus operandi* response to wounds from friendly fire was self-condemnation. I could quote Romans 8:1 "There is therefore now no condemnation to those who are in Christ Jesus." But I felt the hidden evil of my heart demanded reprisal. Already prone to self-debasement, my imagination added other sins to whatever wickedness was discerned by the elders. It was a short leap to believing I was the vilest person that ever lived, and I heaped upon myself derision and scorn. Eventually, I would have to cease from this self-flagellation from sheer exhaustion.

My indulgence in self-condemnation was akin to bloodletting. Spiritually, mentally, and emotionally, I cut myself with knives of self-loathing and hate. Did I have to engage in such self-defeating behavior? No. No one forced me. It was my choice, my unhealthy reaction to disapproval. The force of my backlash was an indication of the flame of my desire for fame and acclaim. My lust for recognition manifested in visions of greatness. Many mornings I awoke with a picture in my mind of being on a stage wowing an audience with my brilliance. Truth gradually corroded that image, but, even then, there was more work to be done.

People in Jesus' day followed Him for different reasons. Those drawn to the deliverance ministry also came for different reasons. There were Nicodemuses who came with inquiring minds; Peters, Jameses. and Johns who came for the demonstration of power and words of eternal life. There were Marys and Susannas, Marthas and Josephs. I came as Mary Magdalene out of whom Jesus cast seven devils. Not that I literally had seven devils, but many deeply embedded crooked ways, some generational, did, indeed, bedevil me.

Was I and my fellow soldiers ignorant, misguided souls? Arguably yes. But we showed up. And at the end of the day, Jesus cares most about the heart and its motivations. I believe people who wrestle with the real issues of life, attempting to make a difference for righteousness' sake, deserve respect. I find comfort in these words from Teddy Roosevelt's "Man in the Arena" speech:

> It is not the critic who counts; not the man who points out how the strong man stumbles, or where the doer of deeds could have done them better. The credit belongs to the man who is actually in the arena, whose face is marred by dust and sweat and blood; who strives valiantly; who errs, who comes short again and again, because there is no effort without error and shortcoming; but who does actually strive to do the deeds; who knows great enthusiasms, the great devotions; who spends himself in a worthy cause, who at the best knows in the end the triumph of high achievement, and at the worst, if he fails, at least fails while daring greatly, so that his place shall never be with those cold and timid souls who neither know victory nor defeat.

I and my fellow soldiers were definitely in the arena, marred by dust and sweat and blood and striving valiantly for the dream of purity in Christ.

Chapter 14 | **The Drifting**

To look at my daughters' faces in the rearview mirror as I drove away from the Mission was torment. I left my family. I left my friends. I was alone and I was afraid. I checked in to a Super 8 Motel in Rochester and hid. No one, not my family, not my co-workers, knew where I was. In my mind that was safety. I went to work at school, came home and hid.

I spent Thanksgiving in my hotel room, telling myself, "It's okay to be alone on Thanksgiving, you're safe because you're hidden. The world is dangerous. The world is against you. God is against you and you deserve every rejection, every punishment."

I didn't have to be alone; I could have called Howard. Though we had been separated for three years I knew Howard held no animosity towards me. He would have allowed me to move in with him. Economically, it made sense. I was 59 years old and had never been entirely financially independent without some possible back-up.

Anxiety rose in my mind.

Do I have what it takes to make it on my own?

After a couple months living in the motel, I had to make a decision. I could not forever hide away. For hours, I sat in the lobby of the Super 8 motel trying to hear from God. The entry-level salary I was earning at the Montessori school wouldn't go very far. If I returned to Howard it would only be for monetary expediency. With his covetousness still strongly influencing him, finances would be grounds for arguments, and I would be subject once again to his control.

Finally, I chose to fling myself towards God and God alone. I didn't know whether He would catch me. It was time to find out if I trusted Him and if He was worthy of trust. There was no one to ask for advice. I wouldn't have trusted any advice given anyway.

In fear and trembling, I rented an apartment close to my job. I did not tell my family where I was. When they called, I did not answer the phone. My apartment became my new cave of withdrawal. Within its walls, alone, I had a measure of peace. There I continued my self-imposed, self-righteous path to redemption -- fasting, writing scripture, listening to Bible on CDs.

Choosing to isolate myself was painful, but I believe it was the best decision for both myself and my family. An angry, wounded animal is a danger to well-meaning people who try to give it aid. I was bitter for failing in my quest for holiness and deeply wounded by self-inflicted condemnation and hate. My family would have tried to help, and I would have vehemently rejected their overtures of kindness and hurt them even more. As the saying goes, hurt people, hurt people.

At one of the last prayer meetings I attended at the Mission someone quoted Hebrews 10:31 (ISV), "It is a terrifying thing to fall into the hands of the living God!"

I replied, "That's what I want." Desperation precluded fear. Whether I lived or died, I wanted to duke it out *mano a mano* with God.

Leaving a ministry I had been involved in for 34 years rocked me to the core. My marriage was gone, and my family was at arm's length. I blamed myself for losing everything that had provided stability and meaning to my life.

If the godliest saints I knew with all their wisdom and power had failed to help me become a faithful follower of Christ, then I am irredeemable. I don't deserve to live.

Not only was I without value, I believed I was a force for evil. God had thrown me to the scrap pile. I was worthless.

The cry of my heart from the time I was saved came from the lyrics of an old gospel song, "Jesus, use me, and please, Lord, don't refuse me. For surely there's a work that I can do. Even though it's humble, help my will to crumble, though the cost be great I'll work for You." But in my tormented thoughts, God had refused me. I was an outcast to the Kingdom of God and even worse, an evil force in society. The thought of living the rest of my life with no hope of redemption was unbearable.

Darkness covered my soul akin to my experience years earlier in the basement of the Mission. This time there was no dependent infant to compel me to choose life. I felt like I was floating aimlessly in the blackness of space, tethered to nothing.

Sleep eluded me those long winter months. Every night the endless hours in my reclusive exile pushed my mind into thoughts of suicide.

I could walk into Lake Ontario. It wouldn't take long before I lost consciousness.

Loneliness is a breeding ground the enemy of our souls uses to create separation and crush hope inside the heart. Satan's thoughts have easy access to the mind of a person who feels lost and alone. Persuaded that no one understands your plight you reject proffered help.

In the deliverance ministry we believed, rightly or wrongly, that we were on the front lines of the spiritual battle between good and evil. We were saving our nation and the world. I condemned myself for abandoning my friends and fellow soldiers in the heat of battle. Soldiers who go AWOL in time of war are shot without question, without mercy. How could I explain that to someone who wasn't there? No one would believe me. They would try to talk me out of my self-hate, and they would be wrong. I was a deserter and a traitor. I deserved to die.

Religious exercises of fasting, listening to the Bible on tape, copying scripture, Spirit-led in the past had brought life to me. Now those activities were dry as dust. My unstable mind believed only the "wrath of God poured out on the wicked" scriptures. I rejected the promises and blessings in the Word because they no longer applied to me.

Week after week, month after month I put my energy into this useless, Pharisaical pursuit of favor with God. I was barely functional as a teacher in the classroom. Every evening and weekend I withdrew into my self-imposed cell of solitary confinement. I didn't understand the debilitating effect on the soul that comes from burrowing into such a deep and dark space until Howard called me one evening. Previously I had rejected all phone calls from family. But after six months, Howard had become the hound of heaven. When I didn't answer his calls, he phoned the school and disrupted my class.

To prevent that embarrassment, I began answering

the phone when he called. This time he chattered on and on about shopping for groceries, what he ate for breakfast, what came in the mail. As he talked, tears began rolling down my face. The sound of another human's voice, even the voice of this man, was comfort, a lifeline thrown into the dungeon of my despair.

"And I will give you the treasures of darkness..." (Isa. 45:3). The Hebrew word translated darkness, *choshek*, also means *misery, sorrow, ignorance*.

In that dark place God gave me a treasure: "It is not good for man to be alone" (Gen. 2:18 KJV). That passage in Genesis refers to God creating Eve to be a helpmeet for Adam, but the truth of that scripture was confirmed to me in a different context. With Howard's phone call I knew, with a certainty that only experience can give, that it truly is not good for a human being to dwell alone. People need people. I had withdrawn from life thinking I was doing myself and everyone else a favor. I thought in rejecting life I could save myself from sinning, from making mistakes, from failing.

"Truly, I tell all of you emphatically, unless a grain of wheat falls into the ground and dies, it remains alone. But if it dies, it produces a lot of grain" (Jn. 12:24 International Standard Version).

To the perfectionist, being human is a kind of death. Embracing our humanity means trying, failing, learning, accepting. I worshiped my own idol of perfection — an idol that never makes a mistake. A god. I was chasing the lie of Satan told to Adam and Eve in the beginning, "You can be gods" (Gen. 3:5).

True worship is accepting what God created us to be, grains of wheat sown into this earth experience. If we remain encased in the shell of our own system of self-preservation and refuse to live the life God gives us, we will abide alone, no matter how many people surround us. If we chose, again and again, to die to a protected life, to the life we think we want, we discover our true selves, the selves that God hid in Christ (Col 3:3).

The final breaking of my Pharisee shell came in a church nursery. Walking into that local church I had a plan.

I know how to be a Christian — serve in the lowest place.

Although these people had never seen me before, the nursery staff accepted my offer of help. I held the babies, fantasizing that I was earning spiritual medals. As the end of the service drew near, a young man asked me to pray.

I gave it my best shot and the man rhapsodized, "Wow... Wow! What knowledge! What wisdom! We all should just sit at your feet and learn from you."

For a few moments, his words were a balm to my wounded soul.

Finally, someone who sees value in me.

Then awareness came. The balm was poison. That man was throwing garlands of worship at the feet of my idol and I was receiving them as my due. God used that man to hold up a mirror to my soul and the picture showed me my Pharisee -- ugly, gnarled self-centeredness masquerading as Christian service.

I laid down the baby I was holding in my arms and ran home as fast as I could. I was undone. I ceased all religious activities. Except for an occasional glance, I stopped reading the Bible, stopped listening to Bible CDs, stopped copying scriptures. I did not return to that church or any church for many months. The facade of my identity, who I thought I was, had been dealt a death blow.

Summertime. I didn't know how I could face another year in the classroom. My boss, Sally, knew I was struggling and tried to reach me.

I rejected all her words of hope and encouragement until she said, "Karen, don't throw your life away."

In an instant, I was transported back to the Mission standing in front of the dumpster. "Karen, don't throw your life away." The Spirit's words arrested me then.

The same words spoken by my boss arrested me again. Sally continued, "With some people, I know when their season with us is over and I release them, but not you. God told me to hang on to you."

Chapter 15 | **Re-Entry**

The message from the Holy Spirit, twice repeated, was clear. I needed to retrieve my life from the dumpster of rejection and self-hate the way I had retrieved my Montessori notebooks from the dumpster at the Mission.

How? Truth. "Then you will know the truth, and the truth will set you free" (Jn. 8:32 NIV).

The summer of 2007 I spent hours walking in the park and hours in the local library. Browsing through the philosophy, psychology and religion section, I ran across Eric Fromm's book, *The Art of Loving*.

> The practice of the art of loving requires the practice of faith.[3]
>
> Faith requires courage, the ability to take a risk, the readiness even to accept pain and disappointment. Whoever insists on safety and

security as primary conditions of life cannot have faith. Whoever shuts himself off in a system of defense, where distance and possession are his means of security, makes himself a prisoner.[4]

The courage of despair is the opposite of the courage of love.[5]

Eric Fromm provided the first key of truth, to unlock the door to my cage of misery. His accurate description of my spiritual and mental state stunned me. I had insisted on safety and security. I had even considered quitting my job, moving in with Howard and lying in bed curled in a fetal position.

One thought had stopped me — my children. They would be so disappointed if I made myself a prisoner. It was contrary to everything I had taught them about life.

Embracing the courage of despair and wrapping it around my soul like a shroud was my misguided attempt to both protect and save myself. I had begged God, "Please let me die for my sins." I was desperate to assuage my guilt.

God replied as an employer to a job applicant, "That job's already been taken. My Son died for your sins 2,000 years ago, Karen. The only job opening available to you is live. Live for Me."

I humbled myself and accepted Jesus as my Savior all over again. We are not only saved once, we are saved every time we cry out, "Jesus, help me."

Another key of truth came from Graham Cooke's prophetic word, *The Inheritance*.

> Thus says the Lord, "It is your job to be loved outrageously. That is why I chose you, that you would live as one outrageously loved. I will love

you outrageously all the days of your life, because I don't know how to be any other Way.

"I come to set you free from how you see yourself. When I look at you, I see someone I can love outrageously. I have so much to bestow on you, so many places to take you in My heart, but you can't go there unless you allow Me to love you. My love will bring every wall crashing down."[6]

I had been trying to convince God that I was unlovable. I certainly believed it. All my mental, emotional writhing, all my hurling accusations at Him and myself were futile unless I could get Him to accept the premise that I was unlovable. I may have convinced myself, but I would not change the character of the Creator of the universe. Father God is love and He has chosen to love me. I could receive His love or reject it, but I could not alter it.

With the acknowledgment of the truth of God's love came the acceptance of another truth. All my life I had been chasing the dream of attaining an exalted position as a Super Spiritual Woman. That pedestal does not exist in the kingdom of God. It's a mirage, a lie from Satan. Believing the truth removed the blinders from my eyes. I began to notice, appreciate and enjoy the life I had instead of dissipating my energies chasing after a life that could never be. It was time to come out of my cave of isolation. It was time to re-enter life.

My first concern was the classroom. The new school year would begin in a few weeks.

Even if I have failed utterly and completely, I know God has invested a lot of time teaching me what's good for children. He sent me to conferences and a variety teacher training programs to immerse me in several streams of educational thought. I may not make any spiritual progress myself for the rest of my days. But this day I make a vow. I vow before God and all of heaven to do everything in my power to give every child in my care the tools for success in this life and the next.

That decision proved to be a turning point. Convinced God wanted me in the classroom yet fearing failure I pondered, *How am I going to do this? I am so empty.*

In spite of years of training and successful teaching, at that moment I felt totally bereft. What path forward would serve to both energize me and impart knowledge to the children?

The Spirit spoke five words to my mind, "God so loved the world..." (Jn. 3:16).

I experienced the love God has for this Earth. It was like I was in outer space beside God, hovering above Earth. I felt His love for the dirt, for the mountains, for the animals, for the oceans, for everything. I was amazed. I didn't know God loved His creation so much.

Geography is an integral part of the Montessori curriculum. Puzzle maps of every continent occupy a prominent space in the classroom. With the love God imparted to me for His Earth I created a curriculum focusing on one continent per month. I read books about the animals native to that continent. We studied the topographical features and made maps with sawdust playdough, construction paper and colored pasta.

I purchased a CD created by a husband and wife team who put to music the names of every continent and their countries. The children learned the songs and we all danced to the music. I scoured thrift stores for linen tablecloths and china. The older children cooked cultural dishes, set the tables with linen and china and invited their parents for a luncheon celebrating the continent of the month. The love God imparted to me for His world spilled out onto the children.

    South America was our designated continent of the month in October. The song naming all the countries in South America that we sang daily was catchy and easy to learn. Once we completed each month's study and moved on to another continent, I did not review the previous ones. A mom was cooking chili for supper one evening in April when her four-year-old son, Aiden asked, "Mom, what are you cooking?

    "Chili."

    Aiden snorted, "Mom, Chile is not a food, it's a COUNTRY!" Five months after Aiden had heard any reference in class to Chile and South America, he showed himself as a geographer extraordinaire.

    Aiden's parents had presumed to send him to public school for his Kindergarten year to save paying the tuition of the Montessori private school. That one incident changed their minds. They were so impressed with Aiden's fertile and expanding brain power they sent him back to my class and paid private school tuition instead of sending him to public school as they had intended.

    Seeing the world through the lens of God's care brought streams of life to the classroom and to the desert of my soul. My new found joy in geography spilled over into other areas of study and the children were infected by my zeal. As my students discovered more about the Earth, I discovered more of my own identity. I was God's creation — a being who could experience His love for something as humble as dirt and pass that love onto others.

    I began to see the children in my classroom through renewed eyes. They were people — each one unique, special, with his own thoughts, persuasions and beliefs. Realizing the enormous privilege I had of holding up a torch of truth for these children, I took pleasure in their company.

Eric Fromm proposed, "If I love, I am in a constant state of active concern with the loved person. Loving actively cancels out boredom." [7]

I proved that to be true. When I practiced the art of loving, every moment in my classroom became a moment I was alive and free.

Fromm writes that to grow in love one must live a disciplined life and love a disciplined life. He maintains, "The art of loving must begin by practicing discipline, concentration and patience throughout every phase of life."[8]

I finally understood. Where before I feared and hated discipline, I now loved it. I embraced it. I danced with it. My new love affair led me to create situations in my classroom to develop self-discipline in the children.

Learning about sonoluminescence, the production of light from sound, was a revelation I applied to learning. God created the world by projecting His voice through the virgin watery mass saying, "Let there be light" (Gen. 1:3). The human brain is 90 percent water. God's voice passing through our brain produces illumination, truth, ah-hah moments.

Jesus taught, "My sheep hear my voice, and I know them, and they follow me" (Jn. 10:27 KJV).

If I trained the children to obey my vocal commands, I was sensitizing their ears and their spirits to hear the voice of Jesus and follow Him. That possibility fired my imagination.

I instructed my students, "The more disciplined you are the more fun we can have. If you always obey my voice, I can trust you to be safe and we can have multiplied adventures outside."

Recalling Michael Pearl's book and example I made obeying my voice a game. The designated leaders for the day were given instructions. "You may go ahead of the rest of the class if you stop and wait at that tree. If you fail to stop, you will lose your leadership role because I cannot to trust you to obey my voice and keep us safe."

The children rose to the challenge and grew in self-discipline. We took excursions no other pre-school classes dared to take trekking ¼ mile or more to parks and to the horse corral. We hiked nature trails to observe birds, bugs and plants. They rolled down hills, raced around the school's pond and searched for tadpoles.

My number one goal for every child had always been academic achievement. Being a convert to discipline I vowed, *This year training in self-discipline is my number one priority. These children might leave my classroom dumb, but they will be disciplined.*

To my surprise, focusing on discipline improved everything, including academics. Later, I realized that, of course, academic achievement soared. Apply discipline to any endeavor and excellence is assured. I finally understood, not only with my head, but with my heart, that discipline is not a synonym for hate, torture and cruelty. Rather, discipline is a key ingredient of love.

My new freedom made it easier to "not sweat the small stuff." Laughing at my own mistakes brought compassion and understanding on other's foibles. I had reconnected with reality and I felt sufficiently healed to rejoin my family.

The reuniting was gradual — first with Joy, Lois and Susanna. Six months after I departed from the Mission Joy and Susanna also left and shared Lois' apartment. They did not suffer the same condemnation in being sent from the deliverance ministry.

The pronouncement to them was, "You were born into this ministry and way of life and it's the only life you know. It's time to explore, grow and test your wings in the larger world."

I saw them occasionally and spent Christmas of 2007 with them. Joy and I took a road trip to Indiana to pick up Rachelle from school. While she drove, I read C. S. Lewis' "Mere Christianity" aloud and we laughed. Exclaiming and marveling together about Lewis' brilliant exposition made the miles go swiftly and reignited our love for each other and for our shared fellowship in Christ.

Complete reunion occurred nearly two years after my exodus from the deliverance ministry. Sam and Bevin needed a summer babysitter for my three grandchildren. I felt restored sufficiently that I volunteered for the job. That small outreach created a bridge. Holidays and summer picnics and pool parties followed gathering us together as a family again.

My children are now more precious to me than ever. I know the pain of being without that vital bond. I saw Howard at family functions, spoke to him on the phone when he called and occasionally went out for a meal with him. We had been separated for six years. Emotionally, I continued to hold myself aloof and distant. I did not trust him. I did not trust myself with him. Could I, or should I, let down my walls of self-protection and let Howard in?

Chapter 16 | **Life After Death**

The possibility of connection with Howard came when I finally accepted the fact that he was not going to change. He was seventy-five years old, ruling his own life with no outside demands on his time or money. Still inflexible and at times actually mean, Howard was prone to make unreasonable demands on whomever was around. He showed little to no interest in his children or grandchildren. At one family Christmas gathering he showed up at 6:00 pm after everyone had gone home because he was too busy to come any sooner. Nevertheless, there no longer existed a valid reason for me to be afraid and distant. Howard posed no threat to our now grown children. If he began to exert unwanted control when I visited, I could grab my keys, pick up my purse and walk out the door.

    I had no desire to live with Howard again. To meet my expenses, I was teaching full-time and had two small part-time jobs as well. I worked seven days a week and had no time or energy to fulfill the standard wife role of cook, house cleaner and laundress.

My image of what a Christian wife is supposed to be, however, made me feel guilty. If I was a true Christian I would live with my husband. That internal pressure drove me to investigate the possibility of renting a house near my work. I went so far as to contact the owner and bring Howard for a walk through. It was a barn of a home, large and uninviting. Space was required for Howard's stuff. His penchant for collecting had grown into a near hoarding condition and I knew he would not throw anything away. Renting this house would cost more than what we were each currently paying and stretch our combined incomes to the max.

Guilt almost pushed me into renting this house. Thankfully the Lord stopped me with a question. "You don't like the living arrangement I have made for you and Howard?"

The Father went on to explain: "You are both in good situations that meet your needs. Howard is in a small house, easy to keep warm and comfortable in cold, New York winters. And you have an apartment suited to your current circumstance. You have a romantic, fairy tale vision of what living with Howard again would be like — all white picket fences, sunshine and roses. Let me tell you what it would really be like. Howard will take over the entire property with his stuff. You will have a small bedroom to yourself and that is all. The house is large and drafty and for the five months of winter you and Howard will be confined to a few small rooms. Plus, it costs more and would be untenable financially."

I repented of my folly. Guilt-driven religion can bring you to the brink of disaster while you think you're doing what's right. Thank God He is a present help in our time of need, because I needed a swift reality check.

Children, naturally, want to see their parents together. No matter the reasons for separation, that hope lingers in the hearts of most children.

I was grateful when Jonathan commented, "Mom, I'm glad you didn't go back to Dad." Jonathan's words confirmed God's will to me. They put me at ease, and I felt comforted in Jonathan's desire to protect my heart.

Howard and I began vacationing together. The first time came about in August 2009. Desperate to get away and having a longstanding aspiration to visit Maine, I first contemplated taking a trip alone. That prospect did not seem like much fun, so I dared to call Howard.

"I'm driving to Maine tomorrow. Do you want to come with me?"

So anxious was I to escape I would have left that afternoon, but I knew Howard needed a minimum of twenty-four hours to adjust.

"Hold it, hold it. Yes, I'll come with you, but we don't have to leave so soon." He was still the voice of reason and steadiness to my impetuosity. In the spirit of compromise, I gave him two days instead of one to prepare for the impromptu adventure.

We got in my car with no agenda other than to drive up the coast of Maine and visit some lighthouses. We meandered for three days, purchased a ride on a sailboat at Bar Harbor, visited Winter's Gone alpaca farm in Wiscasset and climbed a mountain. This mountain was situated on an island in the middle of a lake, accessible only by boat. Howard heard about the fantastic photo opportunities that were to be had on top of this mountain from a fellow photographer at the motel where we were staying.

Since we were on "Howard time," we didn't arrive at the boat launch until 2:30 p.m. When the boat crew dropped us off, they informed us the last boat left the island at 6:00 p.m. Walking the trail along the shore, we came upon two signs, one pointing to an easier three-and-a-half-mile trail to the summit and one indicating a two-mile, more challenging hike. Since we were already running late, we chose the two-mile trail.

A few hundred yards into the woods the trail narrowed to a path nearly straight up the mountain. Howard led the way, pulling me up over boulders, charging up the hill like a man in his prime. I, 14 years younger, was gasping for breath and barely keeping up. When we arrived at the top, I collapsed on the ground. Convinced I did not have the strength to walk back down the mountain I announced, "I'm staying up here with the bears and the moose tonight." As I lay moaning on the ground, Howard climbed the two flights of stairs on the tower to get his pictures.

It was now 6:00 p.m. We were at the top of the mountain and the last boat was scheduled to leave the island. Howard encouraged me, "I'll descend the mountain as fast as I can, maybe I can catch the boat. You come when you feel up to it."

After another five minutes I struggled to my feet and with wobbly legs and rubbery knees began my unsteady downward trek. I let gravity pull me, using my legs only as brakes.

Fortunately for us, the boat owners knew we were still on the mountain and had waited. As I neared the bottom of the hill, the boat with Howard in it rounded a curve in the shoreline. Howard stood up and waved enthusiastically. I dragged my sore body into the boat for the ride back to the mainland.

Howard was up early and ready to roll the next morning. I was still so sore and exhausted I stayed in bed declaring, "I'm not going anywhere today."

We were genuinely enjoying ourselves. Our Maine trip proved that I could adjust myself to Howard and still have fun. Some of the irritating triggers of our former relationship I infused with peace.

When we had children and schedules Howard was often the one not ready on time. It had been a great source of distress for me. Now, with no deadline to meet, no children needing assistance I picked up *The Omnivore's Dilemma* by Michael Pollan to continue reading. I was in a most delightful part of the book as Michael experiences life on a farm. I read excerpts to Howard as he readied himself for the day. It was more than mere tolerance. I was genuinely enjoying this opportunity to reconnect with Howard, and I was very grateful that peace could replace irritation.

On the Saturday after we arrived home from Maine, Howard felt ill and broke into a sweat. Even though he was suspicious it was his heart, he did not seek medical care for two days. Typical. Driving himself to the VA clinic Monday morning, the staff promptly took him to the hospital by ambulance as an EKG confirmed he had suffered a heart attack.

I disbelieved what I was hearing from the doctors. "His coronary arteries are 75% blocked," they announced.

How could that be? My husband had just demonstrated the vitality, strength and stamina of a man half his age.

But the report was confirmed. Howard did have a heart attack. Perhaps, if he had been hospitalized right away, there could have been a better recovery. As it was, congestive heart failure was the diagnosis with diuretics and blood thinners the recommended course of action.

Howard hated drugs. He took his prescriptions for a

week or so after leaving the hospital then left them on the kitchen counter, claiming the pills made him feel like committing suicide. He researched natural alternatives and doctored himself with herbs. But the Howard Rode self-medication program was insufficient. His heart was not strong enough to pump the fluids out of his body and his legs began to swell. Then the skin ruptured in open sores and water poured out. It was back to the hospital for a ten day stay to drain the excess fluid from his system.

    For the next three years Howard and I took more vacations. We toured Israel with Jonathan Bernis and Jewish Voice Ministries, something Howard had wanted to do since his twenties. We drove along the St. Lawrence River and ended up at Laura Ingalls original home in northern New York. We spent a week at a health retreat in North Carolina. About once a year Howard ended up in the hospital again to drain the excess fluid out of his body. Exertion made him gasp for breath because fluid would build up around his lungs.

    I was in New Jersey at a wedding when I received the call. Sam had discovered Howard disheveled and disoriented at home. He was taking him to the hospital. After tests and evaluation, the doctor informed me, "Howard's legs are full of blood clots. Any one of them could break loose at any time causing death. We could continue to perform more procedures. They would be painful, possibly avert death in the short term, but not for long. What do you want us to do?"

    I called Sam. He called Nate. We made the decision to suspend treatment and place Howard in hospice care. Our children, who were scattered across the country, flew home to say goodbye to their Dad. Two days after our 40th wedding anniversary on July 18, 2012, Howard passed away.

A memorial service was attended by family and a few friends. Through the miracle of technology, family who had returned to their work were Facetimed in. Spontaneously, the children shared what Howard had meant in their lives. It was surprising and gratifying to me what they held dear.

Nate testified, "What I learned from Dad is patience. When he was helping me work on my car and I was getting frustrated because I couldn't figure something out, he said, 'Don't get upset. That clouds your mind. Just keep looking for the solution and it will become apparent.'"

Miriam credited Howard with bringing her back to God. After his heart attack she realized her dad wouldn't be around forever, so she often joined him in church just to spend time with him. Having distanced herself from anything church related after the rift with the Mission, Miriam at first was irritated by the church service. But gradually words of truth and love softened her heart. She eventually joined a small group and became friends with the assistant pastor.

Jonathan recalled an overnight encampment trip, sleeping on the USS Little Rock at the Naval and Military Park in Buffalo, NY. This trip was planned by our home school group, and Jonathan was grateful for that weekend of personal time, just he and his dad.

Joy was required to go to work with Howard one day because all her brothers were busy. Having heard detailed accounts from her siblings of Howard's dominating, critical demeanor on the job, Joy braced herself for a difficult day. However, Howard was kind and patient with her. The day that began with dread ended with a precious memory of spending quality time with her father.

I was captivated by the warm memories my children

shared. I concluded that part of the service with these words, "Despite the struggles, I have no regrets. The best thing your Dad and I ever did was have you kids. You children are your Dad's and my greatest treasures. You are what made our lives worthwhile and meaningful. I'm grateful your Dad and I had these past few years to take trips, enjoy each other's company, and experience reconciliation. I did not expect that we would ever bridge the chasm that seemed so wide when we separated. God showed us such mercy. I'm so glad there was peace between us at the end."

After I dispensed with the paperwork and legal details of Howard's passing, I incomprehensibly fell into depression. The world lost all its color; I saw only gray. Motivation to do anything eluded me.

Why am I still here? I have nothing to live for.

I was totally unprepared for this reaction to Howard's death. It would be understandable if ours had been a loving, interdependent relationship, but I had not looked to my husband for emotional, financial or any other kind of support for many years. I was bewildered.

School would start in a few weeks. Carrying this gray cloud of hopelessness into the classroom would not do. It wouldn't be fair to the children. *God, please, help me.*

King David wrote, "He sent His word, and healed them, and delivered them from their destructions" (Ps. 107:20).

God sent me Ecclesiastes 11: 4-6 (AMP):

> He who observes the wind [and waits for all conditions to be favorable] will not sow, and he who regards the clouds will not reap. As you know not what is the way of the wind, or how the spirit comes

to the bones in the womb of a pregnant woman, even so you know not the work of God, Who does all. In the morning sow your seed, and in the evening withhold not your hands, for you know not which shall prosper, whether this or that, or whether both alike will be good.

God spoke to my heart, "Karen, get out there and live your life." The cloud of doom dissipated.
That's right! You never know what God's going to do. Something wonderful might be just around the corner. I wouldn't want to miss that! Two years passed before those prophetic words, "Get out there and live your new life," came to fruition in an unexpected way.

Chapter 17 | The Wild Atlantic Way

In June of 2014, at age 67, I retired from teaching. It had been two years since Howard's death. Two years since God had pulled me out of despondency with the admonition to, "Get out there and live your life." Living my life in those years revolved around teaching. During the school year I worked at the Montessori school. Summers and vacations, I gathered my preschool grandchildren together and taught them. My goal and expectation in retirement was to be available to my daughters and daughters-in-law, to help in any way I could with my grandchildren.

Four weeks after school ended, I idly browsed YouTube videos and I came across a message by musician and teacher, Ray Hughes. I hadn't watched anything of Ray's for months and, in fact, had forgotten about him. On a lark I listened. I almost closed down the video when Ray finished preaching.

Oh well, I'll let the video run to the end.

It was those last few minutes that would change my

life. Ray announced, "We're going to Ireland, ya'll. Look up Awestruck Tours on the internet, sign up and come with us."

Ray's message was recorded in March, so I knew the tour he was advertising had already taken place, but I was intrigued by the name "Awestruck Tours."

I'd like to be on a tour with a name like that.

I typed "Awestruck Tours" in the search box and the internet took me to Sloan Travel's website.

A sidebar on the website announced the next tour: Exploris Tour to Ireland September 19-30, Scotland, England and Wales October 1-10.

Ancestors on my mother's side had Scottish heritage and Jonathan had sent me a lavish "retirement, Mother's Day, birthday" gift of $5,000.

Why not go? I have funds. I'm retired. My ancestors came from Scotland.

With the tour mere weeks away, I expected it to be sold out. I emailed tour owner, Coty Sloan, expressing my interest in traveling to Scotland. By the time Coty responded a few days later my imagination had already taken me across the Atlantic. When Coty called to tell me the tour to Scotland was full but there was one spot open on the Ireland tour, I took only seconds to consider.

Ireland is almost to Scotland. Close enough.

"Sign me up."

I had never considered Ireland a tourist destination. It wasn't on my radar. If I heard of others making a trek to Ireland, I mused, *Whatever for? What's in Ireland?*

The only tours I had been on were bus tours and I imagined myself filling the last seat on Sloan Travel's tour bus. I was stunned when Coty informed me this was a private tour with just four ladies, two of them also retired teachers.

Airline ticket purchased, bags packed, I flew from Rochester, NY to Dublin where Coty promised to pick us up. As I flew, I prayed. It had been years since I had traveled out of the United States. This trip was to a nation I never intended to visit, with people I had never met, in a small entourage with no chance of being invisible in a crowd. I was a little anxious. I hoped this adventure was ordained of the Lord.

Too late now. With the Atlantic Ocean under my feet, there was no turning back.

I arrived in Dublin, got my bags, and walked out into the airport lobby. There stood Coty, holding a sign with my name on it, arms open in a welcoming hug. He handed me a gift bag filled with Irish candy and cookies and a Celtic style journal. Such a warm welcome melted uncertainty. Courage rose. I walked into the Irish sunshine, senses alert, eager to experience all this trip had in store for me.

Rendezvousing with the rest of the crew at the airport, I met Judy, Sandy and Jennifer. With luggage piled high in the back of the van, we set out for our 11-day journey. First stop was the Rock of Cashel, the largest castle ruin in Ireland. Ancient ruins such as castles and abbeys feed my mind. I marvel at the engineering feats, the astounding craftsmanship, the ornate carvings, but it is music and nature that feed my soul and spirit.

I stood outside this 1,400-year-old castle on a hill and looked out over the countryside. My eyes feasted on sun-dappled rolling hills, pastures arranged like a crazy patchwork quilt, and distant mountains sheltering the plain. Contentment flooded my soul. This scene proved to be a mere appetizer to the lavish banquet of beauty that was to be laid before me in the days ahead.

An entree of music was added that very afternoon.

As we drove to Ireland's west coast, Coty played his *Melodies of the Spirit* album — a collection of violin melodies he had composed and recorded.

How could a 30-year-old young man create music that is so soothing and healing to a 67-year-old like me? I was enthralled.

The next day, we hiked along the Cliffs of Moher followed by a boat ride to view the cliffs ocean side. I wrote in my journal, "What a spa day does for the body, each day on this tour does for my soul and spirit. I am fully satisfied, fully nourished in mind, body, soul and spirit. Oh, the wonder of it all."

One of my favorite Bible verses is Psalm 145:16 (NIV): "You open your hand and satisfy the desires of every living thing."

Every day in Ireland God was opening His hand and satisfying my desires. I was living, breathing, experiencing that scripture that had been so precious to me for so many years. Gratitude engulfed me.

Continuing along The Wild Atlantic Way, we stopped in the picturesque city of Galway and walked around while Coty shopped for groceries. Piling into the van, grocery bags squeezed into every corner and beside our legs, we drove to our next destination -- a house at Kilbride Point. This new home situated in the wilds of Connemara sat at the end of a dirt path overlooking Lough Mask.

Spending three days in the Irish countryside at a house on a lake with no other houses in view? What could be better? Trees, lakes, country lanes and sheep grazing in pastures drew me outside early every morning. I walked along the dirt road filling my soul with the richness of nature and my stomach with wild blackberries that grew on the fences. It was heaven. The richness of provision for my soul was matched by the richness of Coty's cooking of hearty meal-in-a-bowl potato soup. We were immersed in Irish natural beauty and cuisine.

I had purchased a small, travel-size New Testament to take with me to Ireland. It had been eight years since I left the deliverance ministry, seven and a half years since I had read much of the Word. The scriptures had become such a book of condemnation to me, that I hardly opened my Bible. My fourth day in Ireland, while overlooking Lough Mask, I wrote in my journal, "I want to read the Word. I haven't wanted to for years!" A love for God's Word was restored to me in Ireland and that love abides with me to this day.

One of the verses that spoke to my heart was Psalm 142:5 (AMP): "I cried to You, O Lord; I said, You are my refuge, my portion in the land of the living." It is a wondrous comfort and blessing when the Holy Spirit breathes life into His Word and makes it relevant for that very moment.

By nature, I am an introvert and I seldom initiate conversation. My tour mates were more loquacious, peppering our travel times with comments about the weather or the quaint cafe where we ate lunch or our scenic stops. They asked Coty questions about Irish history, the tour agenda, the pubs, the music.

As I listened to my tour mates' pleasant exchanges, I feared they might think me uppity or aloof if I did not contribute something to the conversation. Every so often, I spoke up - not because I had anything of note to say, but just to let these strangers know I enjoyed their company and was not being standoffish.

I wrestled with this dilemma for several days. The Holy Spirit illuminated Matthew 6:1 (AMP) to my mind.

"Take care not to do your good deeds publicly or

before men, in order to be seen by them…"

Jesus asked me, "Are you going to talk just to be seen by your tour mates because you are afraid of what they might think? Or are you going to be at peace being silent unless or until you have something to contribute to the conversation?"

Scripture is alive and speaks to daily life in the here and now. I was released from the pressure of pretending to be a garrulous extrovert when in reality I am the opposite. The Spirit freed me to be me. It was a first step through a doorway of exploration into my true self in Christ that continues to this day.

From Kilbride Point we toured Cong, stopped at a Woolen Mill and walked a nature trail. The flying of falcons is a guaranteed perk on a Sloan Travel tour. What a treat to have those magnificent creatures perch on my arm, taking off and landing, and a double treat that the falcons are housed at Ashford Castle.

A nearby cottage was the setting for the movie, "The Quiet Man," starring John Wayne and Maureen O'Hara. Memorabilia from the movie fills the living room of this cottage. The lady of the house was a child at the time of the filming. Her recollection of those days fascinated us, and she showed us John Wayne's suitcase that the actor had gifted her father with when Wayne left for America. We returned to our lodging and watched *The Quiet Man* that evening. Ever thoughtful, Coty had purchased the movie especially for this occasion.

Coming home from a *Trad on the Prom* performance of Irish dance and music, Coty played his vocal CD, *Anchor of Hope*. I didn't know our tour guide was a singer/songwriter in addition to a violinist.

Sitting in the back seat of the van, the music and lyrics washed over me in ever increasing waves of love.

"The Sea That Forgets," "Solace in the Night," "Monet."

How could this man, in his youth, write songs that so powerfully express my heart?

By the last song, "I'm Yours," I was so overcome with emotion I felt wasted at Jesus' feet. Seemingly swept up to the throne of God, I was overcome and undone by this intimate moment with Jesus. The passion I experienced in previous profound encounters with the living God had always dissipated by morning. I expected the same with this incident. But this time was different. The enriched spiritual atmosphere lingered on like a permeating fragrance.

Throughout the rest of the tour — Kylemore Abbey, Slieve League, Giant's Causeway — I felt held in especial nearness to the Lord. Coty drove us to the longest beach in Ireland. We spent an hour taking pictures, writing in the sand and watching a man harness his horse to a racing cart and guide him through the waves. The cliff above the beach held the ruins of Downhill Estate.

As I stood at the edge of the rock face gazing out over the Atlantic Ocean the majestic scenery filled me to overflowing. It was achingly beautiful. My heart hurt. My soul, my mind, my heart was too small to contain the glory of God's creation. So enraptured that I had no adequate words, I wanted to run, I wanted to shout, I wanted to express what I was feeling inside.

The final day of our tour took us to the Titanic Museum. It was news to me that the Titanic had been built in Belfast, Northern Ireland. A full-size replica of the bow of the Titanic loomed above us as we entered the memorial. The underwater scenes of the actual ship, the reconstruction of events, the biography of survivors and victims take the visitor back in time. It is a sobering reminder of the disastrous consequences when the pride and arrogance of men blind them to danger. One cannot leave unmoved.

Checking into our downtown suite on the 26th floor we relaxed, enjoying an impressive view of Belfast through the floor to ceiling windows gracing two sides of the living room. As we ate dinner at McHugh's pub we each reminisced on what event of the tour most engraved itself on our minds and hearts. It was a difficult choice. All of the trip had been so glorious. Flying falcons soared to the top of everyone's list, but for me standing on the cliffs of Downhill Estate and Mussenden's Temple eclipsed even the rapture of flying Harris hawks. The sense of touching original creation resonated with something deep within me. It called to me, beckoning me to seek out the purpose for which I was created.

The following morning Jenn and I were scheduled to catch an early bus to Dublin for our flight home. As I lay in bed, I adjusted and readjusted my thoughts. I didn't want to rob myself of the pleasure of the last remaining hours on this life-altering trip. Neither did I want to fall off the cliff into depression when I returned home. I shored myself up, exhorting my inner person, "Prepare for the loss of this heavenly experience. Brace yourself for a downshift to your plain and simple life."

Chapter 18 | **The Mount**

Back in Rochester, I returned to my usual activities of driving twice a week to pick up my pre-school aged grandchildren and bringing them to Joy's house for school. I taught Sunday School and chauffeured Rachelle to worship team practice. My day-to-day routine remained much the same, but my inner life felt brand new. The baptism of love, glory and intimacy with Christ I experienced in Ireland had changed me. Even my children noticed. I had been touched by glory and I would never be the same.

After Howard's passing, I purchased an Ani L'Dodi ring that bore the inscription in Hebrew and English, "I am my beloved's and he is mine." I wore it to keep my love and commitment to both Howard and the Lord fresh in my memory. It was a sweet token that I wore after Howard died. So revitalized was this post-Ireland life that I purchased a Claddagh ring to commemorate my trip and consigned the Ani L'Dodi ring to a drawer. The glory of

God's presence in Ireland, like a tsunami, had engulfed me. I was swept away from the trickle of small expectations into the sea of God's limitless possibilities.

    In an attempt to explain to myself this extraordinary and unforeseen turn in my life I looked to times in my past where I had also felt the presence of God in an unusual way. Years previously I was embroiled in an internal crisis concerning Howard. I had come to the conclusion that his zeal to follow Christ flagged. My thoughts were born more from fear than fact as Howard had not yet turned inward to self-promotion. But this was a resident fear from my teenage years. In declaring my resolve to follow Jesus I had avowed, "I'd rather do life alone than have to drag somebody with me."

    It is true that if your spouse doesn't share your passions, life together can become strained. The Bible instructs, "be not unequally yoked" (2 Cor. 6:14) for good reason. One person's resistance can be like an anchor thrown overboard on a boat you're trying to paddle across the sea. I believed this was especially true if the person resisting is the head of the family. All my striving meant nothing if I couldn't motivate Howard to retrieve the anchor and pick up his oar.

    At that juncture my belief was based on fear rather than fact. I had no evidence of Howard's backward slide except a difference of opinion on something Pastor Ben had said. I sided with Ben as a matter of loyalty and spiritual survival. Howard wanted me to stand with him and challenge Ben. I refused. The deliverance ministry was my hope of heaven. If Howard, my head, turned away in the slightest, it threatened my and our children's security. Fear persuaded me that all was lost.

    I'm done. I quit. I will no longer exert any energy or effort to run after God. I will not seek Him. I will not pray.

God knew that deep down I meant it.

A few nights later baby Susanna awoke in the early morning hours to nurse. Instead of rolling slowly out of the covers as usual the Holy Spirit catapulted me out of bed. My whole body vibrated, every cell exulting, "I'm alive with eternal life! I'm alive in Christ!" This supernatural invasion jump-started my heart, rekindled hope and the will to press on. Thank God for His mercy to quell that fear in me then. Soon enough I would live through the reality of Howard's change of heart.

The second divine visitation I described in Chapter 11. A torrent of God's love and power washed over me. I had no understanding at the time. Now believe it was God's grace-filled way of preparing me for the soon coming separation from the Mission. In the years following, despair nearly extinguished the flame of life within me. Every time I was going down for the third time, drowning in hopelessness, the memory of that divine touch was a rock to stand on, pushing my head above the waves. I could not dismiss or deny that demonstration of the Father's love for me.

Those previous close encounters with God had come at specific times for specific needs. But Ireland was different. The fragrance of the encounter in Ireland, like an essential oil, infused my daily life. The aroma, the presence was palpable. There seemed to be a golden hue about each day. It was as if I had been on some kind of Mount of Transfiguration and had a new revelation of Jesus.

I searched the scriptures for answers. *What happened when Jesus, Peter, James and John came down from the Mount?* They encountered the man whose son was demon possessed. Little did I know at that moment, but in the days, months, and years after Ireland, I was to confront two inner demons of my own. Those demons were not literal entities that needed to be cast out. They were attitudes, beliefs buried deep in my soul that needed to be excised. I would need the Mount experience of Ireland to hold me steady.

I shared Coty's music with my pastor which opened the door for Coty to minister at New Covenant Church in January of 2016. I hosted Coty during his visit to upstate New York. One afternoon he worked on the logistics for his 2016 tours to Ireland and Wales.

"I'm trying something new in 2016," Coty explained. "Rather than stay at four or five different locations packing and unpacking I'll book lodging at one central place. It will be a regional tour, taking day trips to local sites."

Coty showed me a few of the options he was considering. One was a Victorian Manor built in 1590. He imagined it would be the *creme de la creme* place to stay in Wales. Ideally situated close to Snowdonia National Park with all attractions a few hours' drive away, the manor seemed beyond perfect. I nodded encouragingly as Coty shared these details.

One not to be missed attraction Coty discovered in his research was Zip World. This adventure park advertised the fastest zipline in the world and the longest one in Europe. Gleefully, Coty burbled, "Riders fly head first at over 100 miles per hour!"

Not wanting to squelch his enthusiasm, I hid my horror. The thought of anyone creating a zip line that would hurtle fragile humans at over 100 miles per hour was shocking enough. That people actually engaged in such lunacy was unimaginable.

Never would I participate in such a ridiculous risk to life and limb!

The following morning on my walk the Lord asked me, "Why are you treating Coty's plans for Wales as if it doesn't have anything to do with you?"

Uh, because it doesn't?

"Think again, Karen. You're going to Wales."

That's impossible! Outrageous to even consider! I'll hold this thought at arm's length, maybe even at toes' length. I'm absolutely not mentioning this to anybody now. Maybe next summer if I think I have the finances, I'll revisit the possibility. Highly unlikely, though.

Again, God spoke, "You're going to Wales and I want you to tell Coty that you're going."

I completed the final leg of my walk, climbed the stairs to my apartment and announced, "Coty, I'm going to Wales with you."

Surprised, Coty responded, "Well, looks like it's time for another adventure, Karen."

This was January, the tour to Wales was scheduled for October, 10 months away. Knowing I was apprehensive about Zip World, Coty emailed me in February, "You must at least consider the possibility of riding the zipline in Wales. You're not too old, too anxious or too fearful."

I protested, "I'm all of the above and a few other things besides!"

But Coty's zeal prevailed, and I promised, "only because I have grown exceedingly fond of you, will I attempt the impossible — ride the fastest zipline in the world." Coty declared he was giving me an eight-month head start to prepare myself mentally. And, being terrified of both speed and heights, the behemoth death trap known as Velocity was never far from my mind.

In those intervening months, God exposed the two demons of twisted thought buried deep in my soul. I ordered Michael Pearl's DVD series on the subject of the brain and addiction thinking it might be helpful to a family member. Since I am not bound by addiction, I watched the DVDs only so I would know what was in them before sending them on. However, after viewing the four-hour presentation I felt compelled to follow the prescribed remedy just in case there was a hidden addiction in me of which I was unaware.

Scientific evidence indicates it takes 40 days of abstinence for the brain to rewire and no longer demand the euphoria addiction brings. Mr. Pearl recommended 50 days of fasting because 50 is the number of Jubilee, when according to Biblical law all captives are set free. I decided to fast from Facebook and all news sources for 50 days.

Nearing the end of the 50 days I was feeling the full effects of the fast -- isolated and on God's rack of discipline. God spoke and exposed the first demon, "You are addicted to an independent spirit. If you don't separate yourself from it, you will miss the calling and purpose of your life on this earth."

I was undone. How could this be? I had obeyed Christ the best I knew how for years. Stunned, appalled, I didn't what to think. But the Lord confirmed that severe word a few days later in Martha Kilpatrick's blog.

> In Eden's Garden the woman persuaded, using clever words to conquer Adam. By mere talk she tore him from his God and destroyed Paradise. Such is the force of words that spew from seductive conversations with Satan. To ponder is our creative joy. To question is no sin. But to make up answers apart from God…that is the potential evil of logic and the inevitable ruin it births.

God gave us a splendid mind so that He would have a volitional companion. He is a 'speaking Father' and relishes conversation.

He delights to be the answer to our questions. And He Himself is the answer. **I AM** knows everything.

Eve ingested a forbidden fruit—**the sweet juice of mental independence**. It turned within her to a poison of forceful domination and **her daughters have inherited its addictive taste.** It was woman vying for God's position over man. And the horror is that she won, by the use of mere words! (Emphasis mine)[9]

How was I to separate from something I couldn't see? Something that was so intertwined in the me-ness of me that I thought it was me? In the midst of this devastating news, I visited my Ireland tour mates in Georgia and my second demon was exposed.

Chapter 19 | **Molech**

In the midst of joyously reconnecting with my friends, God shocked my senses. Sitting at a table in a quaint bookstore, waiting for Judy to complete her shopping, the Spirit spoke.

"Molech."

What in the world?

Molech is an ancient heathen idol referenced in the Old Testament. This idol had hollow outstretched arms heated with fire during festivals. Worshippers sacrificed their children, placing infants on Molech's arms burning them alive. That visual is graphic and disturbing, I know. The Father impressed on my mind that I was guilty of passing my children through the fires of Molech.

I was stunned, horrified.

How could this be? How could there be any parallel between my life and such acts of pure evil?

There is no overt tension between my now grown children and me. We love each other and enjoy our times together. While some would say that love is all you need, God knows the heart and He began to search mine.

I babbled incoherently to Judy in search of answers. She shared a vision God had recently given her. In the vision, she was a warrior mother praying over her son during a difficult season in his life. The Lord showed Judy that her fervent, incessant prayers created a force field of protection over her son holding back the powers of evil.

Days later back home in New York God connected Judy's vision and Molech. God spoke as "Elohim," the Creator. "Karen, never give up your motherhood. It is primal, foundational, part of the fabric of My original creation. No matter how bad the circumstance, no matter how you've failed, never give up your motherhood. Trust Me and I'll bring you through and make everything right."

The Father equated the rejection and abandonment of my children to passing them through the fires of Molech. I gave up my motherhood for a season when I left the Mission. Grievously, that was not the only time.

Throughout my years in the deliverance ministry the elder women had instructed me on how to better love my children. Lydia once said, "The homeschooling, the swimming outings, the tea parties, the sewing, the cooking -- from all outward standards you're a marvel. Anywhere else you would receive accolades. Not here. Here we deal with and expose the thoughts and intents of the heart."

In my heart lay a worm of pride, a hidden motive for it all. I didn't want it to be true, and even now you may read this and not want it to be true. You may think it was one of Lydia's misguided words. It was not. It was true. I wanted exaltation for my efforts, adulation, worship even, from others and from my children. On a conscious level, I understood my twisted ambition, but my heart's bent had remained the same.

After being told in the Mission prayer meeting that my arms and legs were severed from my spiritual body, I became desperate. Rather than pray for a path to healing, I asked Lydia to care for my children, spiritually. I gave my children away. I felt I was an unfit mother. Lydia and the other women apparently knew how to do motherhood right. My children would be better off with them. Lydia did not contradict or correct me. Hers and others' silent acquiescence convinced me this transaction was justified, even noble. After all, I was sacrificing for my children's sake. Though I could excuse my abandonment of motherhood and blame it on others, God was holding me accountable.

At that time, I didn't know God's thoughts about motherhood. I didn't know giving away my children was wrong, and I don't think Lydia or the other women at the Mission did either. There was so much emphasis in the ministry of "Don't control your children," and "Your enemies are they of your own household" that the teaching sometimes got out of balance.

In the aftermath of this prayer session nothing changed at the natural level. I took care of my children as always. But if all dynamics are known in the spirit, my children knew I had given them away. Years later that feeling of rejection and abandonment further embedded in my daughters' hearts the night I left them standing at the doorway as I drove away from the Mission.

As tragic as those incidents are, turning my back on my children didn't end there. Author and teacher, Steve McVey wrote, "When our beliefs become more important than our relationships, grace has left the building." In my zeal to follow Christ wholly and hate any relationship that might come between me and Him, I was guilty of elevating my beliefs above motherly love. I pushed grace from my heart.

When Sharon was living and working in Virginia, I often called her with a scripture or word of exhortation. At one point she had had enough, and lashed out, "Could you just be a Mom for one second and stop trying to fix me! I don't need fixing." I replied, "No, I can't. This is who I am!" I equated being "just a mom" to sloppy agape, compromising the standard of Christian living to accommodate flesh, something the ministry warned about again and again. Sharon was already estranged from Howard at that juncture in her life. My Pharisaical attitude made her feel like she was now also without a mother — an orphan in this world.

The memory of those phone conversations coupled with God's admonition regarding Molech shattered my heart. Fountains of the deep broke up in me and I wailed. I saw no path forward, no salve for what I had done in denying my children the benefit of a fully present mother.

The following morning, I went to church. As I sat in brokenness and regret, waiting for the service to begin, I felt Jesus come and sit beside me. I can't recall another time when His presence as Friend was so pronounced. He comforted me. "I knew this day would come, Karen. This day when you would deeply, deeply regret what you have done or not done. I know your heart. I know you would give your life if you could to undo any of the damage to your children, but you can't fix it. You can't undo what's been done. That's why I came. That's why I died — to do what you can't do. What you can do is join Me. Come with Me and watch Me fix everything. Be My hands, be My feet, be My mouthpiece. I'll show you how to be a better mother to your children."

In the months that followed, I asked my children to forgive me. They offered not only their forgiveness but their understanding. And though my children are now all adults, I committed to being fully present in their lives. "I'm here for you if you need me. I will never again abandon my place as your mother. You children are my greatest treasure, my greatest joy, and I am privileged beyond measure that you call me, 'Mom.'"

The demon of Molech was excised. There remained the other demon, addiction to mental independence. While in Georgia I attended a prayer meeting and shared a little of my testimony. A prophetic word came that I was to write about my spiritual journey. I doubted that anyone would understand or desire to read about the twists and turns of my life. But, having the word of the Lord, I began. I couldn't know that my writing was a setup from God to not only share my story, but also to rescue me from addiction to a spirit of independence.

The Wales tour drew closer and something besides Velocity disquieted me— my arthritic hip. For years, doctors, friends, therapists, and my children had all recommended a hip replacement. In the fall of 2015, my siblings and their spouses climbed on board the "rah, rah" train of encouragement when I joined them for an Alaskan cruise. My family expressed dismay watching me limp around the cruise ship. Sweet, unassertive Laurie, my sister-in-law, quietly urged, "You simply MUST pray through and let the Lord speak to you about having surgery."

Why was I so resistant? Fear. Blessed with good health I had never been hospitalized. Only two times in my life I'd had blood drawn. Both times I fainted. I did not know how to navigate the labyrinth that I perceived our modern medical system to be. Furthermore, I did not know who to trust. I only had Medicare Part A insurance covering hospitalization and no funds to pay for a $40,000 surgery. Worst of all, if I signed up for surgery, it would be scheduled weeks or months in advance. I would be subjecting myself to the mind-numbing fear of anticipated doom for all that time. I just couldn't face it.

Ten days after I arrived home from the cruise, I flew to Los Cabos, Mexico to attend Miriam's wedding. Back home in Rochester with no further travel plans the Lord spoke to me, "I have more places to send you and things for you to do, but I can't send you anywhere until you get that hip fixed."

A word from the Lord is miraculous in its efficacy. Fear subsided and I applied for Medicare, Part B and supplemental insurance. Time constraints on the supplemental insurance policy meant January 2017 would be the earliest possible chance for a hip replacement. The Wales trip was scheduled for October 2016. I puzzled over the timing considering the word I had received from the Lord.

Knowing the upcoming tour to Wales included horseback riding and I loved riding as a child I tried mounting Lois' horse to see if my arthritic hips could handle it. They couldn't. It seemed so simple, just swing your leg up and over like I did as a child. Impossible. I was so disappointed I wouldn't be able to join in that activity in Snowdonia Park.

In the meantime, my brother, Steve, and sister-in-law, Debbie, who live in Wisconsin had hip replacements of their own. Mark Heller performed their surgeries. Dr. Heller has thousands of successful surgeries to his credit. He had performed knee surgeries for my sister, Kim. Debbie and Kim apprised Mark of my situation. "We'll get you through this," they promised. "Fly up here, stay with us, have Dr. Heller do your surgery."

After sorting through her medical bills, Debbie

called me. My cost after Medicare paid its share would be minimal. I could afford to have surgery that summer rather than wait until 2017 for supplemental insurance benefits. Debbie gave me the phone numbers of the hospital's business office and Dr. Heller's secretary. I made two phone calls and in 15 minutes all was arranged. Surgery was scheduled for August 24th, six weeks before my departure to Wales.

True to their promise, Kim, Debbie and the Lord got me through hip replacement surgery. Knowing that God had paved the way so sovereignly allayed my fear. I stayed with Steve and Debbie for two weeks following surgery. Having recently gone through the experience themselves, they were the ultimate caregivers. It was simply wonderful.

A week before my departure to Wales, I again attempted to mount Lois' horse. This time I was successful. The word of the Lord came to pass, "I can't send you anywhere until your hip is fixed." My hip was fixed just in time for my trip to Wales.

I continued to question the wisdom of ziplining at 100 miles per hour. Tape still covered the incisions from surgery and fear welled up within me at every thought of Velocity. I happened on Jason Upton's song, "Fly," on YouTube.

> Going up to new atmospheres, going up to new places...
> Heavenly places...
> God wants to take you to new places,
> New revelation, new perspective, aerial view,
> I declare God has given you the air,
> So fly.
> It's time to spread out your wings,

It's time to shake off the things that hold you down,
It's time to spread out your wings and
Fly, just fly... (Jason Upton, *Fly*)

Such a precise characterization of my soon adventure convinced me that yes, God did indeed want me to fly.

Chapter 20 | **Surprises**

October came and with it Sloan Travel's Snowdonia Sojourn tour. Five of us, Kay, Janice, my son James, Coty and I traveled to northern Wales. Every day was a delight, not just from the places we visited, but in the fellowship we enjoyed with one another.

      The Victorian Manor was, as Coty promised, the *creme de la creme* of lodging facilities. The architecture, the decor rich with original carvings, the fireplaces, the period furnishings immersed us in a time warp. We were transported to the days of castles. Gifts of fresh flowers, candles, candy and a welcome note from Coty awaited us in our bedrooms. His five-star meals awaited us in the dining room. Walking into this setting we immediately felt at home yet at a most exclusive resort. I followed the dirt path behind the manor up into the hills with sheep grazing on either side. The climb culminated in a spectacular view of the ocean.

Yes, this manor is indeed the "creme de la creme."

A few days into our tour we were on our way to Zip World. I was proud of myself for holding my fear in check so far. I had not gone into complete brain paralysis yet. On the drive to Zip World we skirted around mountains and drove by streams. They were spectacular, but inadequate balm to erase my mounting fear. We checked in and the staff helped us into our full body suits and helmets. Traveling at such high speeds requires a streamlined body. The fly suit and gear are designed to hang your body in a sling. Attached to the zipline you fly head first, Superman style, off the side of a mountain. No big deal.

First stop was Little Zipper, which is a 40 mile per hour short run skimming over tree tops. The purpose is to introduce you to the zipline experience, let you get comfortable in your fly suit and give you one last chance to back out of Velocity. The staff said some people do, in fact, back out at this point.

Little Zipper was breathtaking. That's a positive spin for, "I was gasping for breath, fearful I was going to hit the treetops and/or miss my cue to spread my arms to slow myself down and thereby overshoot the landing." None of what I feared came upon me. I didn't hit the treetops. I did open my arms on cue, and I stuck the landing.

We boarded a red utility truck and sat on two long benches for the 20-minute ride to the top of the mountain. Fear surged higher with every minute and I kept telling myself, "Just don't think about it. La-ti-da-ti-da."

My self-medicating strategy was rendered powerless by the Velocity guide's counter drug of choice. He regaled us all the way up the mountain with facts like, "In the first three seconds after launch you'll be traveling at sixty miles per hour hundreds of feet off the ground."

I wanted to yell, "Would you please shut up! I'm trying not to think about it!" It was only because of Coty I had agreed to this idiotic caper. *I might not speak to Coty for the remainder of this trip.*

My second self-medicating plan also failed. Climbing out of the bus at the top of the mountain I strategized, *I won't look at the chasm and where the zip line takes us. I'll focus my eyes in the opposite direction and study the rock formations behind me.*

But, in true comedic timing, our guide called us over to the mountain's edge and pointed into thin air. "See that platform over there? That's where you're headed." That platform, from this distance over a mile away, looked the size of a microchip.

It's official, I'm going to die.

Walking to the launch platform with a dry mouth and jellied knees, all I could think was, *I have to do this, God. I don't know how I'm going to do it, but I have to.*

My brain was almost totally paralyzed now. James sat next to me but that gave little comfort. At go time he would be twenty feet away hooked to his own line. I had to do this alone.

On my hands and knees at the edge of this cliff that dropped off into nothingness the team worked to hook me into place. My weak arms kept collapsing under me as I tried to obey the instructors to hold myself in push-up position. Finally, I was locked on the line with safety checks completed. Feet extended behind me, hands gripping the straps of the sling I looked like Superman. My heart was Chicken Little.

"Three, two, one, launch."

Those first seconds I gasped. Survival was my only goal. The zigzag roads that lead up the mountain grew smaller and smaller as I accelerated to 60 miles an hour.

The ground disappeared; below me lay a beautiful aquamarine reservoir of water.

Time stopped. I entered a realm of absolute silence and calm. Mesmerized, enthralled, overcome, I felt I had broken through the barrier of time and space into eternity. The timeless effect made me think the zipline staff had taken one look at my gray hair and slowed me down. I was traveling over one 100 miles per hour but in mid-air, with no reference point on earth, I felt motionless.

> I have given you wings,
> I have set you free from the things that held you.
> I have given you wings, I have set you free,
> So come to Me,
> Fly.
>
> Like a bird in the air you've escaped the snare of the enemy,
> You have been set free
> Nothing can ever hold you
> Fly, just fly, fly, fly... (Jason Upton, *Fly*)

Thirty seconds later, beyond the quarry, the platform loomed. I approached, caught the shepherd's crook held by a Velocity staff member and was brought to a safe stop. The 60 second ride was over.

So dramatic and instantaneous was my transition from quailing fright to soaring heights that when Coty flew in minutes later, I rushed to him and kissed him on the cheek. I had to tell him I loved this adventure and loved him for seeing past my fear and making me do it.

After the zipline I thought, *No more scary challenges, I can relax and enjoy the remainder of the tour.*

I did enjoy Penrhyn and Harlech Castles, the South

Stack Lighthouse, and St. Bueno's Church. Flying owls and falcons and holding a bald eagle and a golden eagle at a haven for birds was unforgettably exhilarating. Each outing was a smorgasbord of delight for the senses, the finest of the finest. We rode horses in Snowdonia National Park, hiked around a mountain lake and traveled on the train to the summit of Mt. Snowdon, the highest peak in Wales. The stunning scenery everywhere filled my mind and soul to overflowing.

There were two more surprise events, however, that pushed me out of my comfort zone physically. Had I been prepared mentally in advance for these exertions, they would not have disturbed me.

First, was Nant Gwrtheyrn, ocean side site of an abandoned mine. I imagined a short, easy walk over flat ground. Arriving at the top of the path leading to the ocean, I was somewhat dismayed.

Whoa, just whoa. It's a long way down there!

We trekked down to the ocean and wandered around a bit. Then our fearless guide climbed up a gravel hill to the mine ruins, so we followed. I expected the rocks to give way and send me hurtling to the bottom. The rocks held. We stayed a few minutes and James and I gazed out over the Irish sea drinking in the beauty of this place. Coty, seeing a possible shortcut to the very steep path back to the parking lot, charged through head-high weeds. I followed and nearly twisted my ankle and did a face plant on the uneven ground. By the time I reached the parking lot with legs and lungs burning I was a tad miffed by the whole affair.

However, when I climbed into the van joy bubbled up from my inner self and I realized, surprisingly, that the joy was coming from my body. My bones, muscles, heart and lungs were rejoicing in being pushed beyond what I would have chosen to do. It felt good. I thanked Coty a second time.

On to Devil's Bridge Falls. Being a first-time adventure for Coty also, he could not advise us as to the rigors of this hike. We were following Coty on the trail when he turned a corner and burst out laughing. Coming behind him we discovered the reason for his jocularity — Jacob's Ladder — 100 uneven, nearly perpendicular stone steps.

The stairs were so steep that in addition to a safety handrail, a horizontal bar reached halfway across the path every 20 feet. If a hapless adventurer lost his footing and began to tumble down the stairs, he could grab the bar and arrest his fall. Exulting, Coty exclaimed, "These are the steepest stone stairs I've ever seen over here!" *Whoopee,* my mind deadpanned. I gripped the handrail with one hand and gripped James' hand with the other and carefully made my descent.

What goes down must come up. Crossing the bridge at the bottom, we began the ascent. Up and over stairs, some boulder-size, I huffed and puffed my way to the top of the 300-foot waterfall. The scenery -- a swiftly flowing stream, pools and waterfalls nestled in the forest -- was truly breathtaking. Being that close to the torrent was such a treat, but again, it challenged my physical strength and my mind grumbled by the time I finished the climb. A two-hour nap back at the Manor revived both my body and my spirits.

After 14 wonderful days, filled with adventure, sightseeing, laughter, food and fellowship we left Wales. As with Ireland I returned home changed. This time with an infusion of courage. The physical challenges of the Wales tour, with Velocity at the pinnacle have become a metaphor for the future and created a bulwark against fear.

When faced with a decision to embrace risk and struggle or to retreat into comfort and passivity, the memory of my adventures in Wales inspires bravery.

I face winds of change and future unknowns and boast, "I rode Velocity, hiked three miles in the Wales hills, and conquered Devil's Bridge Falls. I can handle anything after that, so life, 'Bring it!'"

Back home in New York I pulled out the pages of my story that I had written in obedience to the prophetic word I received in Georgia a few months previously. Initially, I thought ten pages ought to cover the high points of my spiritual journey, all that anyone would be interested in reading. Stretching myself I managed to pen four chapters before I hit a mental block and couldn't think of anything else to say.

The first chapter, "In a Church Basement," contains lots of drama and I took full advantage of it. My narration began with this line, "If he backs me into a corner, I'll kill him."

That statement could be the opening of a murder mystery. I congratulated myself on the shocking line that was sure to capture a reader's attention. I wrote and rewrote the incident, took it to my writer's group and I received unanimous praise for my suspenseful rendition. I was riding high.

The next morning as I walked down Federal Road where I live the Lord said to me, "Your retelling of that incident is unacceptable to Me."

I clucked and spluttered like a hen doused with water. "No! You take that back, God! I've rewritten this chapter numerous times. Seven people reviewed it and gave me accolades. How could You possibly say it's unacceptable?"

God replied, "You made the man look bad. He didn't

do anything wrong."

The way I set-up the story the reader would have the impression Joe was threatening and aggressive. Actually, he was the opposite. Mild-mannered, in fact. I slandered this good man's character, all so I could write a story with shock value and gain a reputation of being a good writer. The fault did not lie with Joe, but with me.

I complained to my now good friend, Coty Sloan, about what God had said. I told him I had already edited the chapter several times and did not know how to fix it. Coty emailed back, "Send it to me." A half hour later he sent back a revised narrative, the one that is in the book today. Thus began a partnership, me writing, Coty editing. I didn't know that it was a set-up from God to not only to bring about this book, but also to deliver me from my addiction to mental independence.

Coty brought vision, clarity and cohesiveness to my story -- and length. I quit several times -- after chapter 5, after chapter 8, most definitely after chapter 20. What else could I possibly say? Every time I declared, "The End!" Coty laughed! Then he cajoled, encouraged, and assigned more topics to cover. Subtly, without my realizing it, the spirit of independence God had exposed nearly a year previous, began to erode.

A crisis arose when Coty became immersed in his own ventures and didn't comment on the book for several months.

Maybe Coty has lost interest in editing the manuscript. He's been such a help so far, but maybe he's just done. Coty's probably too busy to do anymore. What should I do? Should I forge ahead on my own? Ask another friend to help? Go on Amazon CreateSpace and publish the book myself? Just hurry up and finish it no matter what?

I struggled with this dilemma for several weeks before recalling the Lord's warning 16 months previously. "Separate yourself from the spirit of independence or you will miss My will for your life."

The clean fear of the Lord that is the beginning of wisdom (Prov. 9:10) engulfed me. I vowed, "No matter what pressures I feel I am not moving forward independently. If this book project is never finished, so be it. If it stays buried in Coty's files for months or years, so be it. I am not going to act independently."

That crucial decision broke the back of my addiction to independence. Though I still need to practice and remind myself from time to time, I have learned to value the efficacy of interdependence. When God joins people together in community a synergy is created that produces far more than an individual could accomplish on his or her own. The second demon was excised.

Chapter 21 | **Up from the Wilderness**

"Who is this that comes up from the wilderness, leaning on her Beloved?" Song of Sol. 8:5

I had challenged life, boldly inviting, "Bring it!" What future winds of change could possibly trigger the same overpowering fear as Velocity? Paradoxically, it was the love of God. The light of the Holy Spirit probed the darkness of my lingering doubt that God could really love me. Self-hate and doubt shackled my mind.

In April 2017, I attended a concert by Ernie Haase and Signature Sound. God often uses music as an entrance to my soul. Somewhere around the halfway mark of the concert, just before the bass singer sang, "Old Man River," I sensed a heaviness lift off my shoulders.

I had the thought, "I will never again hate myself." I don't know how and why it happened then, but it has been true to this day. I have not sunk to the lowest levels of that kind of mental self-flagellation since that night. It was a good beginning. More work lay ahead.

Emptying out self-hate left space in my being. With what should fill that vacancy? I could not yet bridge the gap into fully embracing God's love for me. My mind was still too enslaved by doubt and fear. The shackles became obvious when Jesus led me to embark on a new path of self-discovery. The guidance to search out secular venues of self-exploration surprised me. I believed I was already far more introspective than most people. In fact, I considered it one of my faults.

Having no other direction from the Lord, I purchased a copy of the *Learning to Love Yourself Workbook* by Gay Hendricks. Days later I took the online Myers-Briggs personality test, fully determined to decode the mystery of me.

Confirmation came within days of my intersecting with these two streams of thought. As I studied the information suddenly, without warning, fear engulfed me. So overwhelming was this day terror I rushed out of my apartment and hiked three miles in an attempt to escape. It was identical to my fear of Velocity. My fear of ziplining could be explained. This was unreasonable, inexplicable, mind-numbing.

What could possibly incite that degree of dread? My mind was in chaos. I couldn't think, couldn't explain this to myself.

I battled this fear for weeks. Only with concentrated effort could I discipline my mind to continue activities laid out by Hendricks and Personality Hacker. The exercises were helpful and insightful but full understanding did not come until Jesus led me to *The Return of the Prodigal*. Henri Nouwen's book is a character study of the various participants in Jesus' story of the prodigal son.

Nouwen takes us on his own journey through the

story identifying first with the wayward son, then the elder brother, and finally the forgiving father. Those familiar with the story in Luke 15, know the father represents God and we humans, the prodigal son and elder brother.

Rembrandt's painting, *Return of the Prodigal* was the impetus for Nouwen's spiritual pilgrimage. In the painting the prodigal, dressed in rags, kneels before the father. He has lost everything except the remembrance that he is a son. Nouwen writes of his identification with the prodigal.

> It is the place of light, the place of truth, the place of love. It is the place where I so much want to be but am so fearful of being. It is the place where I will receive all I desire, all that I will ever need, but it is also the place where I have to let go of all I most want to hold on to. It is the place that confronts me with the fact that truly accepting love, forgiveness and healing is often much harder than giving it. It is the place beyond earning, deserving and rewarding. It is the place of surrender and complete trust.[10]

I knew that I would never be able to live the great commandment to love without allowing myself to be loved without conditions or prerequisites. The journey from teaching about love to allowing myself to be loved proved much longer than I realized.[11]

We all want love. We spend our lives searching for love. God created man in His own image, which means He created him to love and to be loved. There is no peace until we are safe in the arms of love. Those of us who have trusted in Jesus as Savior have found that perfect love, so why is it so hard for us to receive it and live in it?

What is "the place I most want to hold on to" that Nouwen references? What do I so fear losing that the mere possibility paralyzes my mind, numbs my senses and leaves me quavering in torment? I fear losing my sense of self, the construct of who I believe I am -- in other words, my life. "If you cling to your life, you will lose it; but if you give up your life for me, you will find it," says Jesus (Mt. 10:39).

An altercation with Howard shortly before our separation sheds light on my fear. Howard left the scene of our fight, only to return moments later and ask, "Why do you defend yourself?"

I remained silent but my mind raged, "Because you're trying to kill me!"

That's what it felt like. Years of criticism and domination had shredded my sense of self. I fought back to try to save what little, in my perception, was left of the me-ness of me. It was the instinctive will to survive.

What if I had known then the message of the prodigal? What if I had known "giving up my life for Jesus" meant allowing Him to love me with no merits or worthiness on my part? It may not have influenced Howard's decisions, but it would have brought me a greater measure of peace.

The elder brother in the story Jesus told was the obedient son, outwardly. He didn't squander his inheritance on wine, women and song. He remained with his father, but resentment filled his heart. How this seemingly perfect son really felt was exposed when his younger brother returned home.

The elder brother is a Pharisee. He obeys the law outwardly, but inwardly he is convulsed with jealousy. The Pharisee desires a reputation of righteousness so he can parade his goodness in front of others. He wants to be seen as preeminently good therefore he continually compares himself with others. This results in either condemnation of them or of himself. Bound as a slave to both self-righteousness and self-rejection these mental and spiritual chains "reinforce each other in an ever more vicious way." As Nouwen identifies with his own inner Pharisee he writes,

> Every time I allow myself to be seduced by it, it spins me down in an endless spiral of self-rejection. As I let myself be drawn into the vast interior labyrinth of my complaints, I become more and more lost until, in the end, I feel myself to be the most misunderstood, rejected, neglected, and despised person in the world.[12]

Nouwen describes the Pharisee mindset as,

God isn't really interested in me. He prefers the repentant sinner who comes home after his wild escapades. He doesn't pay attention to me who has never left the house. He takes me for granted. I am not his favorite son. I don't expect him to give me what I really want.[13]

In that expression, Nouwen holds up a mirror to my own inner Pharisee. How guilty I am of thinking the same dark thoughts as the elder brother! God used my children to give me a glimpse of my own version of the cold-hearted older brother.

Spontaneity is integral to my personality. For good or for bad, I eagerly jump onto bright ideas that burst across my mind. When I had a houseful of children a bright idea could send us scrambling to the car for a quick trip to a nearby creek to swim, or to the U-Pick strawberry patch, or to the county fair.

One such idea lit up my brain on Mother's Day, 2017, six months after my trip to Wales. I should have had a premonition that since it was Mother's Day more issues involving motherhood lay ahead. But I didn't. I merrily skipped ahead like Mr. Magoo of cartoon fame, blind to all danger. That Sunday evening, I watched a Derek Prince video in which he taught on the subject of generational bruises and curses. At its conclusion I was inspired to pray one of my "just in case" prayers. Those are the prayers and or actions I take "just in case" it's the right thing to do. So, I prayed for any remaining generational curse to be broken off my children, particularly in the realm of depression or anxiety.

I shared my thoughts and prayers via email with my children inviting them to join me if they wished. Some of my children didn't respond, some of them replied with a simple, "Thanks, Mom."

Others were stirred to confront what, in their estimation, was just another example of "Pharisee Mom preaching to us again. We're completely over it!"

For a week the family email chain exploded with comments, opinions, and revelations. The fireworks provided daily entertainment for the family members who chose to be spectators rather than participants in the action.

When you exert parental authority, hopefully, you have the balance prescribed by scripture. "By mercy and truth iniquity is purged" (Prov. 16:6).

My children informed me I had the truth part down, but I was woefully lacking in mercy. If they came to me with their hurts, I was most likely to offer them a Bible verse Band-Aid and neglect the mercy part. "I'm so sorry that happened. Let me kiss it and give you a hug," was seldom heard from me.

My daughters summed it up this way, "We love you, Mom, but we wish you were more nurturing. If we are in pain, you are not the person we turn to for comfort." One daughter took it even further, challenging the very premise of how I've lived my life. And Jesus concurred. "Listen to your children," He counseled, "They will help you to know who you are in Me."

In my distress at this revelation I reached out to several moms for prayer and counsel. They all agreed, "Listen compassionately without lecturing to your now grown children."

I understood the wisdom of their counsel, but internally I argued, *I haven't said anything directive to my kids in years. In fact, I so honor their independence I rarely contact them. How could I possibly be accused of not listening when there is hardly an occasion to listen at all!*

Jesus intervened, "Yes, Karen, you do listen to your children, but it's with your intellect. I want you to start listening with your heart." He reminded me of several encounters I've had over the past year experiencing the authority of God. It was a realm saturated with absolute protection, security and justice. In that arena of pure love even if the truth was hard to bear mercy walked alongside assuring me that everything would work out alright in the end. By contrast, the realm of my authority was stark, cold, loveless -- built only with truth.

The other comment from my daughter — questioning the premise of my entire life — proved equally illuminating. Thomas Merton observed, "People may spend their whole lives climbing the ladder of success only to find, once they reach the top, that the ladder is leaning against the wrong wall." This thought compelled me to consider that I had never changed my goal from the time I was three years old and proclaimed, "I want to die and go be with Jesus."

To be faced, at 70 years of age, with the possibility that my life's ambition has been wrong all along is shattering. It is akin to Saul traveling to Damascus being thrown to the ground by the revelation of Jesus Christ. As Francis Frangipane so aptly puts it our personal Damascus experience de-masks us to ourselves.

My lifelong goal was heaven, to "die and go be with Jesus." All my striving to be holy was to that end. If getting to heaven is not a valid goal, what is? If I am not to struggle to achieve more and more holiness, how then should I live? What should be my goals? How should I expend my energy? I didn't know. This wouldn't be a mere detour on my planned straight-line trajectory to heaven, it would be a U-turn, a path in the opposite direction.

My daughter counseled, "Determine what you're good at and do that."

That prescription was not new to me. Since retiring from teaching I had ruminated on it with this conclusion, "I'm good with children and old people, so I've been told."

I had worked after school and weekends for Home Instead Senior Care in Rochester and received many compliments for my efforts. In my estimation, I had simply done my job with no fanfare, no extra specials added. Yet older people seemed especially appreciative of my company and my service.

The prospect of caring for the elderly did not appeal to me. Nevertheless, to be obedient to this seeming call to a different way of life, I began volunteering once a week at the local nursing home and took two part-time jobs caring for elderly ladies with mild dementia. Life with seniors is reduced to its simplest, most basic needs. They need help to eat, to go to the bathroom, to walk safely. They need a listening ear and they need to be loved. Which brought me to the third main character in the story of the prodigal son — the father.

The Holy Spirit dropped the idea in my mind to study the subject of jealousy in the Bible. My first reaction was, *Oh, no, that means I'm guilty. I'm going to be found out and condemned for some horrendous jealousy.*

But as I researched the topic, the spotlight did not turn towards me but rather towards God. I became enthralled with the concept that jealousy is synonymous with exclusivity. I contemplated the question, "When do I feel most loved?" When the words, gifts or actions are exclusively, uniquely chosen with thoughts specific to me.

Hearing a generic, "God loves you because He loves everybody the same," leaves me feeling cold and unloved. In my studying this subject I challenged God, "You demand our jealous love towards You. 'You shall worship the Lord your God and Him only shall you serve' and all that. Well, I feel the same way! I feel loved if You, or some person, demonstrates that they know me, my likes and dislikes. I feel loved if they reach out to me in some personal way, showing that I am important and special to them."

I bandied this issue about in my mind over the next several weeks arriving at the obvious conclusion. Although people are incapable of satisfying our very human need to be loved exclusively 24/7, God is capable of extending such love. But I felt there was something missing, something I was not fully understanding. Then I read in *The Return of the Prodigal,* Henri Nouwen's expression of God's jealous love.

In the story, the elder son is angry because he believes the father loves his wastrel younger brother more than him. On the contrary, says Nouwen. It is true that the father ran out to meet the younger son to welcome him home. But when the father knew his oldest son had come from the field and was outside the banquet hall, he left the celebration to go out to that son and invite him into the joyful banquet.

>The joy at the dramatic return of the younger son in no way means that the elder son was less loved, less appreciated, less favored. The father does not compare the two sons. He loves them both with a complete love and expresses that love according to their individual journeys. He knows them both intimately…[14]
>
>The father responds to both according to their uniqueness. The return of the younger son makes him call for a joyful celebration. The return of the elder son makes him extend an invitation to full participation in that joy…[15]
>
>God is urging me to come home, to enter his light, and to discover there, that, in God, all people are uniquely and completely loved.[16]

And isn't that what we all want, what we all long for? Someone to appreciate and value our uniqueness, our specialness? Meditating on that truth has caused me to extend to everyone, especially the senior citizens with whom I have contact, special, exclusive care and attention.

Gradually I am moving from the entrenched thought pattern that my life only matters if I am doing great exploits for God. I am embracing a new thought. That helping a nursing home resident play bingo, heating up a meal, engaging in conversation with one 88-year-old lady who needs a friend matters. I, in a small way, become what

God purposes for us all, to be like Christ. In that place of generosity, that place of "giving myself away" I am moving from fear to love. "If God so loved us *[exclusively, intimately, uniquely]*, we ought also to love one another" (1 Jn. 4:11 additions mine).

What was my mind-numbing fear? I feared to believe, receive, and enter into God's jealous love for me. To believe that I am loved not because of my talent or intelligence or work or anything I can produce, but just because I am -- just because I exist.

"Who is this that comes up from the wilderness, leaning on her Beloved?" It's me. I'm coming up from the wilderness. I'm leaving the land of fear, doubt, and disbelief of the goodness of God. The only escape from such a wilderness is Jesus. I trade my prison of despair, self-rejection and self-loathing for His love. The fierce passion of Jesus' love is stronger than the chains of death and the grave. He has won my heart. It cannot be better stated than in this song of songs composed by King Solomon:

> Who is this one? Look at her now!
> She arises out of her desert, clinging to her beloved.
> When I awakened you under the apple tree,
> as you were feasting upon me,
> I awakened your innermost being with the travail of birth as you longed for more of me.
> Fasten me upon your heart as a seal of fire forevermore.
> This living, consuming flame
> will seal you as my prisoner of love.
> My passion is stronger
> than the chains of death and the grave.
> All-consuming as the very flashes of fire

from the burning heart of God.
Place this fierce, unrelenting fire over your entire being (Song of Solomon 8:5-6 TPT).

Chapter 22 | **This Is What I Know**

"...help us to interpret our lives correctly." (Psalm 90:12 The Passion Translation)

Many times while writing this book, I hit a mental and spiritual crisis or road block. I would reach a place where I was done being vulnerable, done with describing in wretched detail all my faults and failures. Cataloguing my slips and ruinous times so magnified them in my mind that at times it's all I could see. I felt humiliated.

Somewhere between the writing of chapters 19 and 21, I made this accusation against God. *I don't see You requiring this level of soul-baring from anyone else. I understand we connect with people through our vulnerabilities, but 24/7? Am I destined to feel humiliated and low about myself every day? I'm trying to come out of self-hate and self-recrimination, and this is not helping.*

In this distressed state of mind, I drove to Letchworth State Park to hike along the gorge trail. It started to rain and as an even darker cloud approached, I hurried to a close-by picnic pavilion just as the sky opened up. Sitting at a picnic table, watching the torrent create miniature lakes and rivers on the forest floor, I came to the end of myself. Recalling the words of Henri Nouwen that the Pharisee, my persona in that moment, cannot heal himself, I cried out to Jesus:

I can't do this. Mentally, I comprehend the process of transformation -- that You work out salvation in my life little by little, but I just can't do it. I cannot rejoice in the way You expose my failings so You can change them into victories. I still want perfection, not process. I've endured it this long because I held out the perfecting of myself as an achievable goal. If there is no end to process, no end to uncovering my sin and dealing with it, I cannot rejoice. I just can't do this anymore.

As I sat, families and groups of young people sloshed into the pavilion laughing and wiping rain out of their eyes, soaked to the skin. I sat at a table alone and dispirited, unable to enter into the joyous commotion surrounding me.

In that moment, Jesus took me back in memory to my early 20s when I blamed Him for creating male/female function. Jesus said, "Remember when you chose to trust Me then? By faith you accepted My word that My creation and design and purpose for man and woman is good, simply because I did it. You received that truth by faith before you experienced or understood the gift of marriage and children. Remember? Accept the process of My changing your inner self with the same trust you placed in Me then. This transformation of your inner self is a creative act. Just because it's messy, doesn't mean it's bad."

The rain stopped; the sun broke through. I skirted around puddles and dripping trees making my way back along the trail to my car.

I pondered Jesus' correlating inner transformation with the process of birth. Every woman who has experienced natural childbirth can attest to the intensity of that experience. Transition is the third stage of labor in which the body employs the longest, strongest, one-on-top-of-another-with-no-time-to-breathe contractions. This extreme pressure thins the cervix to its maximum to allow the baby entry into the birth canal. There is no stopping or modifying the body's determination to birth the child. It's at that point the mother often feels disoriented, totally out of control, legs shaking and cries out, "I can't do this anymore."

"I can't do this anymore" — my lamentation as I sat underneath that shelter in Letchworth Park. Reflecting on that event, the Holy Spirit likened this reliving my life's story to transition — a laboring of sorts, leading up to a new birth. With that word of encouragement, space opened up in my heart to allow my story to continue to unfold. I pray with David, *"Help me to interpret my life correctly."*

My natural life has been filled with joy, family, beauty, and the fellowship of friends with whom I could share every pain and every victory. Concurrently, my spiritual life has seemed at times full of drudgery, of floating in darkness where understanding and sight were minimal. But, as promised in scripture, God has worked all things for my good (Rom. 8:28). Recollection clarifies my story to me, to understand where I've been and where I'm going.

So, what do I know? What is it that I've learned? Pertaining to the role of men: I have moved from viewing men as a threat to my very existence to a place of honoring them and their integral role in God's created order. I'm no longer that wild Joan of Arc ready to mow down the male species. Dear Lord, it's quite the opposite now. To experience honor in my heart towards men rather than fear is something I cherish as a treasure more precious than gold. It keeps me from ever wanting to hate men again, even when they fail to live up to their calling.

Pertaining to marriage: I know as well as anyone in a difficult marriage honoring your spouse is a day by day, moment by moment battle. Many times, the battle is lost. But some days are joyous, full of love. When we still lived in California, Howard drove our family the 217 miles from Redding to San Francisco. The purpose of the trip was to visit a photography store to adjust Howard's video camera. It turned into a memorable weekend adventure. After visiting the camera store Howard drove us to a park he used to frequent when he was in the Army stationed in San Francisco. The open area with perpetual wind coming off the ocean was a favorite spot for kite flyers. The park was full of people and the air was filled with kites big and small. It captivated us.

Later we drove to the beach and splashed in the ocean. The kids were soaked, and I had no change of clothes for them. The trip was impromptu. We had not planned on staying overnight. Getting dry and warm in a hotel room we turned on the TV and laughed our way through the movie, *The Love Bug*, which happened to be playing.

On the way home the following day, Howard turned off on an unmarked road. It led to a cliff and the launching point for hang gliders. Several enthusiasts were already in the air gliding over the ocean. One man was readying his chute for takeoff. We watched him lift away into the air bending and arcing in sync with the ocean breezes. The entire weekend was such a treat, made even more special by the free-spirited spontaneity of it all. Moments like these were the best of times when Howard and I were in sync. We were one in providing pleasure to our children, one in enjoying life together.

Then there were the other times. The times when one of us poured gasoline on the proverbial fire by deliberately provoking the other. There are a myriad of ways, subtle and blatant, deliberate or unintentional, to block communication and magnify self in a relationship. It takes a lot of cooperative work to tear down those walls and connect in communion rather than strife.

But struggles, joys, hardships, and victories, I'm glad I've been tested on the character challenging arena of marriage — not because I passed with flying colors — I didn't. Though I experienced distress, I still avow, *Father, Your creation of man and woman in the beginning WAS very good just like You said it was. People are not perfect but Your design from the beginning is without fault, perfect in every detail. I've test-driven it and I know it by experience.*

Pertaining to children: Fifty years ago, I regarded children either as aliens from outer space or prospective worshipers of my imagined glory. Now I think of children as gems, each one shining with his or her own unique brilliance. To quote Plutarch, "The mind is not a vessel to be filled but a fire to be kindled." It is a privilege to help light the fire and develop the gifts of God in each child. I've test-driven God's program with children — and also found it flawless. All the ups and downs raising my own 11 children as well as those I taught in my classroom propelled me time and again to Jesus to seek answers. As Jesus promised me years ago, "Children are wings to take you to heavenly places."

Pertaining to discipline: My faulty perception, of equating discipline with punishment, even torture, has been replaced with the truth. Parents who guide their children lovingly along a path of challenge and discipline give them a most important gift -- the knowledge and power to live a successful life. To borrow a term from bowling, parental discipline provides bumpers to a child's life. It keeps him on a straight trajectory and out of the gutter until he is strong enough to chart a direct path for himself.

Pertaining to love: As I reread chapter 22 these months later, I barely identify with the person who wrote those words. Self-hate? An inability to believe in and receive the love of God? The very thought is now so foreign to me as to be nearly incomprehensible.

Chapter 18 relates how I experienced the presence of Jesus as Friend for the first time. Several months later I experienced that same sense of companionship. I had been working extra hours caring for an elderly lady. It was the Saturday, the first Saturday I'd had free in a month and Jesus said, "Let's go out. It'll be fun!" My Scotch nature (both by inheritance and training) reacted with suspicion, "How much is this 'fun' going to cost?" Using gas, putting wear and tear on the car, shopping… all of it non-essential. It had that whiff of sinful extravagance.

But it WAS an invitation from Jesus, so I went. It was one of those superb fall days in upstate New York -- the air brisk and clear, the sky cobalt blue. I spent the afternoon meandering through hills painted orange, red and yellow. Browsing through an antique store I bought Christmas presents for friends and ambled along a nature trail in the Bristol hills.

Taking an alternate route home, I came across a

place I had never visited — The Mill Creek Cafe — a tiny, family-run eatery in the village of Honeoye. I ordered their steak-rice bowl. Steak, black beans, lettuce, salsa, guacamole, and sour cream was heaped on top of rice. Shredded cheese sprinkled decoratively around the edge of the platter with crisp, warm tortilla chips to one side made a delicious late lunch. It was the perfect end to a perfect day — a day spent in wondrous companionship with Jesus. Such peace, quietude and fellowship had been unknown to my ever agitated, ever judging, ever self-critical Pharisee persona.

I didn't want that wonderful day to end and to my surprise it hasn't ended. From that day to this, I have a continuing sense of abiding in the presence of Jesus as Friend. All I had to do was receive His love for me just as I am.

As long as I abide in the most vulnerable place, in the place of truth, in the place of utter need of Him, I am free. When I make my home in that sheltered place in God where nothing is required of me except to receive His jealous, exclusive love, I am at peace, as contented as an infant asleep in safe and loving arms.

Experiencing God's jealous, especial, intentional love for myself makes it possible for me to extend the same to others. That love is unfolding in me like a late summer rose. Not that I claim any degree of perfection, but when I think about it, when I remember to be intentional, I can give consideration, empathy, and love to whoever I am with.

I am reminded of a line from a song in the movie, *Chitty-Chitty Bang Bang*: "From the ashes of disaster grow the roses of success."

That was true for me. A rose bush of love began to grow out of the ashes of despair I felt upon leaving the

Mission. When I relinquished my self-imposed fix Karen program, time, space and freedom opened up to reach a helping hand out to other people. It began with the children in my classroom.

This statement by Eric Fromm was so instructive: "If I love, I am in a constant state of active concern with the loved person...To be fully awake is the condition for not being bored or being boring."[17]

Experimenting in the classroom I found it to be true. The boring work of teaching a four-year-old how to write alphabet letters was transformed into an enjoyable task if I engaged my mind and heart. In observing with love the child's squirmings, his brow furrowed in concentration, I was not bored. I found pleasure in noticing and appreciating the uniqueness of each child.

Every person I come in contact with has a story, a life he or she has lived, a book that he or she could write. Practicing the art of loving delivers me from the arena of viewing people as either potential threats or possible worshipers. Instead, in the words of Henri Nouwen, I experience people and events as "the rich variety of ways in which God makes His presence known to us."[18]

When caring for a woman with slight dementia who sometimes has bathroom accidents, I hold in my mind the image of her as a young woman. Her daughter regales me with stories of her mother spending every Friday and Saturday night at the local hangout feeding nickels into the jukebox and dancing on tabletops.

This transformation of thought, a transformation of me, brings an absoluteness, a surety to my faith. Whether a lesson has been learned or I'm in the process of learning something new, the solid rock I stand on is God's Word. His words have been tried and tested in the furnace of my experiences and have proved to be solid gold.

Chapter 23 | **Changed**

"No matter how empty your life is, to discover the love of God is to have lived."[19]

Martha Kilpatrick

"Let us labor...to enter into that rest" (Heb. 4:11).

As long as we are on this earth, we labor, give earnest diligence, to enter into that rest. What rest? The rest of being one with the Trinity. The rest of being the answer to Jesus' prayer in John 17:21 (TPT), "I pray for them all to be joined together as one even as you and I, Father, are joined together as one."

"Let us." Not "let me" but "let us." We don't make this journey to the kingdom alone. We need a helping hand when we have fallen into a ditch or pitched a tent alongside the path.

I had pitched a tent on the side of the path with regards to motherhood. I plugged my ears and put up a wall making an internal vow: *Nobody better bring up the topic of motherhood to me ever again because I'm not going there. I am so done with scrutinizing my role as mother. I'm as good a mother as I'm ever going to be and that will just have to be good enough!*

So, God sent a fellow sojourner to help me. A friend asked an innocent question about my role as mother. Hiding my true feelings, I gave this friend a non-committal answer but inside I blew a cork. Forced to acknowledge that my vow was not Godly protection but ungodly self-preservation, I reluctantly entered into labor. It was worse than I could have imagined. To the eyes of my spirit this new foray into the issue of motherhood was like facing a volcano filled with the molten lava of fear and doubt expanding and contracting, hissing and groaning like a living monster. My mind filled with dread.

Sometimes you have to plunge to the center of your own earthiness and brave the molten lava there to find healing. The Holy Spirit plunged me into the molten lava of guilt. A friend had written me several years previously, "I see a mother hen with her wings ruffed up and outspread. I think it's been awhile since your children have experienced you as a mother hen in their lives…" That image plagued my mind with guilt like mold growing in a dark place.

And here is an instance where you, dear reader, may be hard pressed to believe me. I know I am not a bad mother. I cooked, cleaned, sewed, protected, educated, and loved my children to the best of my ability. But plunging to the heart, the center of an issue means you leave the reality of the outward display and enter the core.

In the core I found guilt -- mother guilt. There's probably never been a mother who has not felt guilty at some time during her mothering years. It's a cloak we mothers easily wear. The guilt can be traced all the way back to Eve. Can you imagine the thoughts in Eve's mind after Cain killed Abel?

It's my fault Abel is dead, and Cain is a murderer. I listened to the serpent. I persuaded Adam to disobey God. If not for me we'd still be in the Garden enjoying evening walks with God. Cain would know the Lord. He would not have been jealous of his brother. I'm the guilty one. I'm responsible for my son's death.

The light of the Holy Spirit revealed a similar thought process in me. "I killed my children and there is no remedy, no forgiveness."

That's a shocking and untrue statement, yet my heart had reason to believe the lie. I condemned myself for regarding my goal to achieve Super Spiritual Somebody status more important than my children's well-being. That ambition is what drew me to the deliverance ministry.

For some of my children, their experiences in the ministry repelled them rather than drawn them to God. Someone not vitally connected to God is spiritually dead. In the labyrinth of lies in my unconscious mind, I had reached a judgment. I was guilty of killing my children. One could come away from the deliverance ministry believing God was all fire and brimstone. If my children absorbed that image of the Father and rebelled with unhealthy life choices, I carried some of the blame. I was inexorably guilty.

In addition, I could not reconcile what to me were two irreconcilable ideas. My children are now grown and wonderfully independent adults. How can they now shelter under my mothering wings? It's akin to Nicodemus' question to Jesus, "How can a man be born again? Can he enter a second time into his mother's womb?" (Jn 3:4).

Henri Nouwen again came to my rescue. In *The Return of the Prodigal Son* Henri recounts the many lessons the Holy Spirit taught him while viewing Rembrandt's painting.

> The cloak on the father's back "with its warm color and its arch-like shape, offers a welcome place where it is good to be. At first, the cloak covering the bent over figure of the father looked to me like a tent inviting a tired traveler to find some rest. But...another image... came to me: the sheltering wings of the mother bird. They reminded me of Jesus' words: 'Jerusalem, Jerusalem...how often have I longed to gather your children as a hen gathers her chicks under her wings, and you refused!'
>
> Day and night God holds me safe, as a hen holds her chicks secure under her wings...The image of a vigilant mother bird's wings expresses the safety that God offers His children. They express care, protection, a place to rest and feel safe. I begin to see not only a father who clasps his son in his arms, but also a mother who caresses her child, surrounds him with the warmth of her body and holds him against the womb from which he sprang.
>
> Thus, the return of the prodigal son becomes the return to God's womb, the return to the very origins of being and again echoes Jesus' exhortation to Nicodemus to be reborn from above. What I see here is God as mother, receiving back into her womb the one whom she made in her own image. **The divine maternal love is marked by grief, desire, hope and endless waiting.**[20]

No matter what the past has been, anyone, anywhere, man or woman, can extend the maternal love of God for a fellow human being. It is expressed in the outpouring of grief, desire, hope and endless waiting. With the acceptance of that truth the volcano of guilt in my soul evaporated. The saga of my motherhood has come full circle. It began in the heart of God, now it finds its resting place where it began, in His heart.

The Spirit then turned His light on another dark, hidden area in my heart. In January 2018, God again led me to fast, this time from certain foods. I had the uncanny feeling this fast would end with a similar soul revelation as the one two years previous which uncovered the addiction to an independent spirit. I was not wrong.

At the end of the fast the Lord spoke two scriptures to my heart: "Then Jesus said unto them, O fools, and slow of heart to believe all that the prophets have spoken…" (Lk. 24:25) and "How long will you waver between two opinions? If the LORD is God, follow him; but if Baal is God, follow him" (1 Kings 18:21 NIV).

I'm a fool and slow of heart to believe? Vacillating between worshiping God or Baal, a heathen idol?

Stunned, I sought God for an explanation. Understanding came through two back-to-back sermons I viewed on YouTube on the subject of offenses. The challenge from these two ministers speaking in different venues at different times was identical. Do you extend grace, mercy and help to a Christian who has fallen in some way or do you stand aloof so as to not to be seen as condoning his sin?

I would tend to stand aloof in such a circumstance, but the Spirit wanted me to apply the teaching closer to home -- to myself. Do I extend grace, mercy and help to myself when I fail? Or do I berate myself, shower outrage and rejection on my inner being believing such cursing will keep me from falling in the future. That self-adjudicated justice hasn't worked in 70 years.

Could God possibly be equating my offense at my own self as worship of a false god? It WAS the prophets of Baal who cut themselves in a frenzy to bring about their desired goal. What matter if I cut myself physically or mentally or spiritually, I am still worshiping Baal, a god created by human imagination.

The Lord impressed upon me the seriousness of this sin of self-condemnation, by instructing me to give a sin offering. Unfamiliar with the details of the Old Testament sin offering I researched it online.

I found this explanation on First5's website:

> Leviticus 4 deals with the sin offering. The sin offering wasn't for deliberate sins of disobedience. This offering was for an unintentional sin, a sin of ignorance or error. Once a person realized their guilt, they had to confess their sin and present the prescribed offering.[21]

My circumstance fit the criteria for a sin offering. The sin that had not been apparent to me previously had come to a conscious level. I was to make a sin offering immediately after the knowledge of sin was present. Emptying my bank account, I gave a sacrificial offering to a ministry.

"Which of you by taking thought can add one cubit to his stature?" (Mt. 6:27 KJV). All of my striving, all the religious exercise, all the self-flagellation seeking to raise myself up to a higher spiritual plane was for naught. The power of resurrection from the dead resides in God. It is He who raises us up to sit in heavenly places (Eph. 2:6).

Jesus laid out the simple path to freedom: "The truth shall set you free" (Jn. 8:32). The path is simple, but not easy. It is the truth about ourselves and the truth about God that sets us free.

When I pray with King David, "Search me, O God, and know my heart: try me, and know my thoughts: And see if there be any wicked way in me, and lead me in the way everlasting" (Ps. 139:23, 24) and He reveals a gnarled root of sin or pain, unforgiveness or bitterness I have the truth about myself.

Then if I accept the truth of Isaiah 1:18 (ESV), "Come now, let us reason together, says the LORD: though your sins are like scarlet, they shall be as white as snow; though they are red like crimson, they shall become like wool," I am free.

If I am brave enough to look into my Father's eyes instead of inward to my guilt, I find there is no reproach, no condemnation, no rejection. Instead, there is a welcome into His heart where all sin and shame is cleansed and where I am loved, accepted, cherished.

***

In reading my story perhaps you have joined me on this road to the Father's heart. Perhaps you have come to believe if God can do it for me, He can do it for you. The answer is, "Yes, He can." In fact, it's His greatest joy. Your Father rejoices and all heaven with Him when one sinner repents, when one sinner changes his mind about who he is and about who God is (Lk. 15:10).

Your Father has the power to change you and make your life glorious. "... I will make the place of my feet glorious (Isa. 60:13). Your transformed life is at the feet of Jesus in humility, surrender and childlike faith.

A line from one of Edith's songs is both a fitting coda for this part of my journey and a beacon of hope for my continuing pilgrimage. It is the Father's promise to every heart that seeks Him: "I AM your beginning and your destiny. Home and heaven await, but child, your exceeding reward is Me."

The Eleven
Where Are They Now?

Sam owns and operates Rode Homes, Inc. specializing in custom built homes for clients in the Finger Lakes region of upstate New York. His wife, Bevin, is a pharmacist at Strong's Memorial Hospital. They live in Conesus, New York with their 3 children, Dylan, Cameron and Noah.

Nate earned his master's degree in Information Technology from Rochester Institute of Technology. He works as a lead Full-Stack Developer for Freshop, Inc. He and his wife, April, a native of the Philippine Islands, live in Rochester, New York and have two children, Keira and Kyle. April writes a travel blog entitled *Rodes on the Road.*

Miriam graduated from Rochester Institute of Technology and has held a variety of jobs since graduation. Currently, she works as a program manager for Indeed. She and her husband, Don, a Senior Software Developer for The Public Consulting Group, live in Austin, Texas.

James has had a multi-faceted work career as a carpenter, professional ski and snowboard instructor, Emergency Medical Technician, firefighter, and owner of A Colour of Harmony Salon where he currently works as a hairstylist. Basically, James can teach you to ski, put out your house fire, resuscitate you if you suffered from smoke inhalation, rebuild your home, and finish it all off with a color and style job on your hair. He lives in Dillon, Colorado with his three children, Rose, Caleb, and Zane.

Sharon received her bachelor's degree from Virginia Commonwealth University in cross-cultural communication. Following that, she pursued an international master's degree at the European School of Economics with a focus on international communications and marketing in Milan, Italy. She currently lives in Houston, Texas, and works as an advisor of decision quality in the oil and gas industry.

Paul graduated from Rochester Institute of Technology with a degree in 3D Digital Design. He lives and works in Los Angeles, California.

Joy's creative side finds fulfillment in cooking, art, and writing. Joy and her husband, Dan, have four children, Brennan, Kyleigh, Riordan, and Shaelyn. They live in Rush, New York. Joy homeschools her children and works part time at a local market. Dan works as a manufacturing engineer.

Lois is a mail carrier for the US Postal Service. Evenings and week-ends she serves her clientele as a Licensed Massage Therapist. She rides in jumping and cross-country events with her horse, Adagio. Her husband, Derek, works for Rode Homes, Inc. They live in Honeoye Falls, New York with their three children, Ethan, Ariana, and Ivy.

Jonathan loves to travel. After graduating from George Washington University, he acquired his master's degree in business administration through Hult International Business School spending three semesters in London and one semester in Shanghai. Jonathan has toured Europe, Morocco, New Zealand, Australia, Japan, China and several countries in Central and South America. Now settled in Virginia with his bride, Grace, and new baby, Alice, Jonathan works as an IT project manager for Freddie Mac.

Susanna has worked in the food industry and managed the bakery department in a country grocery store. Currently, she lives in Houston, Texas and works for a local retailer.

Rachelle lives in Honeoye Falls, NY and babysits her nieces and nephew while sister, Lois, works. Rachelle taught herself to crochet by watching YouTube videos and sells her crocheted blankets, hats and ponchos at craft shows.

Endnote from the Author

If this book has blessed you in some way and you would like to communicate with the author, Karen can be reached at:

karen.a.rode@gmail.com

References

1 For more information on generational influences see *Breaking Generational Curses* by J. V Hensley. Available on Amazon.

2 John Locke, *John Locke on Education*, Peter Gay, ed. (New York: Bureau of Publications, Teachers College, Columbia University, 1964), 33.

3 Eric Fromm, *The Art of Loving*, (New York: Harper Perennial Modern Classics edition, 2006), 112.

4 Ibid., 116-117.

5 Ibid., 117.

6 Graham Cooke, *The Inheritance*, BrilliantBookHouse.com

7 Fromm, *The Art of Loving*, 118

8 Ibid., 102

9 Martha Kilpatrick, (2014, May 29), "Without a Word," *Read Martha Kilpatrick*, Retrieved from https://readmk.com/articles/without-a-word/

10 Henri J. M. Nouwen, *The Return of the Prodigal Son*, Anniversary Edition, (New York: Convergent, 2016, 17).

11 Ibid., 18.

12 Ibid., 84.

13 Ibid., 98.

14 Ibid., 94

15 Ibid.

16 Ibid., 95

17 Fromm, *Art of Loving*, 118.

18 Henri J. M. Nouwen, *You Are the Beloved,* (New York: Convergent, 2017), 26.

19 Martha Kilpatrick, *Why Am I?* (Loving God Series, Schulamite Publishing, 2009), 10.

20 Nouwen, *Return of the Prodigal*, 116-117.

21 Krista Williams, "The Sin Offering," *First5*, Retrieved from https://first5.org/plans/Leviticus-Hebrews/ff_levheb_7/

Excerpts from *The Return of the Prodigal Sone: A Story of Homecoming* by Henri Nouwen, ©1992 by Henri J.M. Nouwen is used by permission of Doubleday Religion, an imprint of Random House, a division of Penguin Random House LLC. All rights reserved.

Excerpts from *The Inheritance* by Graham Cooke are used by permission of Brilliant Book Publishing. All rights reserved.

Excerpts from *Without a Word* and *Why Am I?* by Martha Kilpatrick are used by permission of Shulamite Publishing. All rights reserved.

Made in the USA
Columbia, SC
04 May 2019